Book of
Garden Wisdom

Also from Random House Value Publishing:

The Old Farmer's Almanac BOOK OF LOVE

The Old Farmer's Almanac

Book of Garden Wisdom

Cynthia Van Hazinga
& the Editors of
The Old Farmer's Almanac

Gramercy Books
New York

This 2000 edition is pubished by Gramercy Books™, an imprint of Random House Value Publishing, Inc., 280 Park Avenue, New York, NY 10017, by arrangement with Random House Books, a division of Random House, Inc.

Gramercy Books™ and design are trademarks of Random House Value Publishing, Inc.

Printed in the United States of America

Owing to limitations of space, all acknowledgments of permissions to use illustrations will be found on pages 210-11.

Random House
New York • Toronto • London • Sydney • Auckland
http://www.randomhouse.com/

Library of Congress Cataloging-in-Publication Data

The old Farmer's almanac book of garden wisdom / Cynthia Van Hazinga and the editors of the Old farmer's almanac.
    p. cm.
   ISBN 0-517-16297-0
1. Gardening. 2. Gardening—United States. I. Title: Garden wisdom. II. Van Hazinga, Cynthia. III. Old farmer's almanac.

SB453 .O39 2001
635—dc21

00-062233

8 7 6 5 4 3 2

To my mother,
- - - - - - - - - - -

Sylvia Wartiainen Van Hazinga,
- -

whose enthusiasm for nature
- -

ignited my own.
- - - - - - - - - -

ACKNOWLEDGMENTS

I would like to thank my three editors — Georgia Orcutt, Sandy Taylor, and Sharon Smith — and all our colleagues and collaborators, especially Benjamin Watson, who contributed sidebars to the book. I appreciate the help of the New York Horticultural Society, especially for the use of its library and the assistance of Kathryn Powis, librarian. Thanks also to the New Hampshire State Library and its staff; the New York Public Library; and the Fuller Public Library in Hillsborough, New Hampshire.

A book has many parents. Thanks also to David Rosenthal of Random House; to Carol Jessop, who designed the book; to Mark Corsey, who did the art research; to Candy Gianetti, who checked the facts; and to Barbara Jatkola, who copy-edited the text.

CONTENTS

INTRODUCTION

"TO PLOW, TO PLANT, TO HOE,

IS THE WORK WHICH LIES BEFORE US NOW."

— *THE OLD FARMER'S ALMANAC*, 1882

Researching and writing this book has led the author and the editors of *The Old Farmer's Almanac* into close contact with our horticultural past and added to our respect for the experience and wisdom of those Gardeners Who Have Gone Before. The journey also has given us a strong sense of nature's enduring patterns, those forces that guide gardeners. For the gardener is only nature's meddling assistant, at best a caretaker of the earth's resources, connected to the process and part of the plan.

Again and again, in compiling our book of advice, anecdote, and observation, calling on tradition and lauding innovation, we were reminded that nothing is new under the sun. Some of the most venerable directives, whether offered in 1828 or 1909, parallel the latest research. Thus, when the 1882 edition of *The Old Farmer's Almanac* advises, "We ought to raise more seed, and not pay so much for what we know so little of," the seed savers of 1996, newly awakened to the importance of the global gene pool and the need for biodiversity, nod emphatically. In 1849, *The Old Farmer's Almanac* reported, "The world, now-a-days, is divided into Conservation and Reform, that is, the old and the new, and so it is in farming." Today ecologists battle developers on the troubled border between civilization and nature, and gardeners use down-to-earth methods on skyscraper roofs.

And now, as then, gardening is a prime recreation and a source of great joy, even as it feeds us. Gardening is a growth industry — growing like a weed. Some gardeners see it as a lifestyle (uniforms by Smith & Hawken) and some as a calling. We are gardeners because we garden; we practice a craft that is both an art and a science; we garden instinctively and knowingly, by tradition and inspiration. As we cultivate and plant, we learn from nature; as we weed and prune, we fill our lungs with air, train our ears to the songs of the birds, and perhaps lower our blood pressures, as the new breed of horticultural therapists asserts. "Flowers have a refining influence," *The Old Farmer's Almanac* noted in 1893, "and never lead astray, but always upward to what is purer and better." Perhaps.

At any rate, as gardeners, we are part of nature, part of civilization, and wholly ourselves.

THE OLD FARMER'S ALMANAC
BOOK OF GARDEN WISDOM

CHAPTER ONE

PLANTING

"A GARDEN IS NOT A LITTLE THING; BUT NEITHER IS IT A SUBJECT FOR SOPHISTICATED CONVERSATION. IF YOU REALLY WANT TO DRAW CLOSE TO YOUR GARDEN, YOU MUST REMEMBER FIRST OF ALL THAT YOU ARE DEALING WITH A BEING THAT LIVES AND DIES; LIKE THE HUMAN BODY, WITH ITS POOR FLESH, ITS ILLNESSES AT TIMES REPUGNANT. ONE MUST NOT ALWAYS SEE IT DRESSED UP FOR A BALL, MANICURED AND IMMACULATE.

"A GARDEN IS, ABOVE ALL, THE HUMBLE EARTH. . . .

"THE SIMPLEST PEASANT, THE LOWLIEST GARDENER, KNOWS DEEP INSIDE HIMSELF THAT THE EARTH IS NOT ONLY THE TRUE SOURCE OF MAN'S LIFE, BUT ALSO HIS PEDESTAL. LET THOSE WHO DON'T LIKE TO DIRTY THEIR HANDS THINK ABOUT THIS: LET THEM CONSIDER THEMSELVES A LITTLE LIKE THE SACRIFICIAL PRIEST, HANDS RED WITH SACRED BLOOD; LET THEM THINK EARNESTLY ABOUT THE OFFICE THEY WISH TO FULFILL. THEN, HAVING LEARNED TO REPRESS THEIR FEARS, LET THEM CAREFULLY WASH THEIR HANDS; THEY WILL THEN FEEL LIKE THE PUREST OF MEN."

— FERNAND LEQUENNE, *MY FRIEND THE GARDEN*

WHERE WOULD WE BE WITHOUT EARTHWORMS?

And do they really whistle while they work?

As you turn over your garden soil, stop and rest now and then — and look for worms. For they are the real plow horses of fertility. "It may be doubted," Charles Darwin wrote, "whether there are many other animals which have played so important a part in the history of the world, as have these lowly organized creatures." Darwin, some researchers have concluded, considered earthworms of greater value than horses, more powerful than African elephants, and even more important to people than cows. Even so, as author Jerry Minnich notes in *The Earthworm Book*, Darwin did not give the earthworm credit for what is now considered its most important function: incubating within its digestive tract enormous quantities of microorganisms, and then casting them off to become the basis for humus.

It is amazing to think that before European settlement, there were essentially no earthworms in North America. Eleven thousand years ago, the Ice Age stripped the planet nearly bare of earthworms. They existed only in a narrow area that included the world's three great agricultural valleys: the Indus, the Euphrates, and the Nile. The soil was rich and fertile in these three river valleys, crops grew almost without cultivation, and great civilizations grew up as well. (In those days, earthworms were appreciated; Cleopatra decreed them sacred, and Egyptians were forbidden to kill them.)

In that same period, few regions in what is now the United States supported extensive agriculture. The Native American population was sparse, widespread, and largely based on hunting and gathering. According to Minnich, "Before European contact, the only lumbricids [the common American and European earthworm is *Lumbricus terrestris*] native to the United States were some lazy species of *Bismatus* and *Eisenia*, essentially worthless as soil builders."

So what happened? Immigrant earthworms (and their egg capsules)

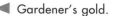

Not-So-Humble Humus

The same Latin word gave us both the noun *humus* and the adjective *humble*. But the contribution of humus to ideal garden soil is anything but humble. Humus is a colloid, a coarse mixture between a solution and a suspension. It can hold water in amounts up to 75 percent of its volume. Humus is the reason good soil can be held in the hand without running through the fingers, why it crumbles like chocolate cake, and why it drains well but holds moisture.

In the moisture are essential minerals, processed, prepared, and served up by microbes for the use of plants. They neither evaporate nor leach away; they contain a feast, a plant's picnic ready to spread in the form of a soft, dark loam that is rich in organic matter and nutrients. Like most ideals, ideal soil is rare, but soil is always improving itself. Any soil can be helped along with humus — that is, its composition can be manipulated to suit the gardener's requirements. After all, in the long run, the soil makes the plant, and the plant makes the soil.

Think of humus not as feeding plants but as feeding the soil itself.

THE CIVILIZED GARDENER

Gardening, or the cultivation of fruits and flowers, may, in some sort, be regarded as the test of civilization. It diffuses peace, contentment, and happiness, stimulates and invigorates the mental and physical powers, promotes habits of industry and domestic frugality among the humbler classes, and places within their reach a large amount of luxury in the shape of delicious fruits and magnificent flowers.

— *THE OLD FARMER'S ALMANAC, 1850*

crossed the Atlantic wedged into the shoes of colonists' horses and packed into the root balls of plants the immigrants brought. Earthworms work fast; soon New England meadows were lush, the Midwest was a vast garden, and fields of grain stretched across the continent.

Earthworms produce more compost faster and more easily than any other organism. As they burrow (constantly eating and excreting) they are bathed in a mucus that stiffens the walls of their tunnels. The tunnels in turn aerate and moisten the soil. Omnivorous and unfussy eaters, earthworms consume nearly everything in their paths — including sand and minerals — as they propel themselves powerfully through the earth.

When they have digested everything and excreted it, the gardener is again the beneficiary. Worms neutralize their own castings (with three pairs of calciferous glands near their stone-grinding gizzards) and deposit them on account in the soil bank with five times the available nitrogen, seven times the phosphate, and eleven times the potash of anything else in the top 6 inches of soil. (They dig down farther than that, too, going as deep as 15 feet, helping to drain the earth.) Castings are totally available organic humus, and every earthworm produces its own weight in castings every day. This can amount to 5 tons of castings on 1 acre of land in a year. And as if this were not amazing enough, some researchers report that earthworms whistle while they work.

One devotee of *Lumbricus* lyric opera, C. Merker, wrote in the 1940s that earthworms have voices and can actually sing in "a definite and changing rhythm" by deliberately opening and closing their mouths. Although they have no lungs, Merker could hear them sing up to 12 feet away, and much of the singing may be in search of love — for worms have five sets of double hearts and meet to copulate in good weather, producing almost two hundred offspring annually. Like the microbes, their companions under the soil, the more organic material they encounter, the faster they reproduce.

Which is lucky for us. Because whether they're singing or silent, where would we be without earthworms?

Note: For further fascinating facts about earthworms, see Jerry Minnich's *The Earthworm Book* (Rodale Press, 1977) and Peter Tompkins and Christopher Baird's *Secrets of the Soil* (Harper & Row, 1989), from which we learned much. ☀

Cleopatra declared earthworms sacred, and Egyptians were forbidden to kill them.

▼

Gardener, Know Thy Soil

Old-time farmers knew that the types of plants that flourished in a particular area gave strong clues as to the type of soil to be found there. Look to the plants that do well, they counseled, and you'll learn as much about your garden as any modern soil test can tell you. As usual, they were right.

Soils that are acidic give root to trailing arbutus, trilliums, buttercups, chamomile, rushes, and mare's-tails. Azaleas indicate acidic soil, as do rhododendrons, camellias, and magnolias.

Blackberries, raspberries, and blueberries grow strong in acidic soil. So do ferns, chrysanthemums, and most lilies. Many plants from woodlands and wetlands — including oaks and pines — are accustomed to acidic soil. Potatoes and many other common vegetable crops prefer it.

Thriving local species often provide clues to soil content. For example:

Type of Plant	Likely Type of Soil
Burdock, chicory, saltbush, wild iris, wild onion	Alkaline
Buttercup	Wet
Ferns	Heavy, possibly clay
Fireweed, nettles	Fertile, moist

Once you know what you've got, just adapt the soil — or your choice of plants — accordingly.

One giant tater, clearly satisfied with its soil.

A HEAD-START PROGRAM

When starting seeds indoors, plant them in anything from seed blocks to eggshells.

I t's a question of timing. Seeds started indoors can get a jump of 4 to 6 weeks on crops sown in the ground. In regions with short growing seasons, this means a great deal. In their vulnerable seedling stages, indoor plants have less competition from weeds. And it's less expensive to grow your own seedlings than to buy plants from a nursery.

HEAD STA

Gardeners start seeds successfully in all sorts of containers and go to great lengths to coddle them at this vulnerable stage. Some plant in pellets, cubes, or peat pots; some use paper or plastic cups, wooden flats, or recycled cans. Our grandmothers used eggshells.

Moisture is the ruling principle at this point. Gardeners using moisture-wicking peat pots or paper bands must take special care not to let them dry out. It's also important to watch for the way the roots are forming. Seedlings grown in pots or flats lose some root strength when they are cut apart, and those grown in individual pots develop circular roots that take a good while to recover.

For strong, healthy seedlings, try soil blocks, available through garden supply catalogs. Container and growing medium all in one, each 2-inch soil block is made of compressed potting mix, a bit wetter than most, which contains a good quantity of fibrous material. Roots fill the soil blocks to the edges and then stop, so that when blocks are set out in the field, seedlings become established quickly and without trauma.

With any kind of container, start seeds in a premoistened potting soil mix. Press them firmly into the soil, then cover them with glass or plastic (a plastic bag works well) and keep them warm until they sprout.

Above all, indoor seedlings need light — a sunny, south-facing window or the benefit of fluorescent lighting equipment. Give seedlings 14 to 16 hours of light a day and keep them moist. Once they have a second set of leaves, they will need a weak solution of fertilizer. ☀

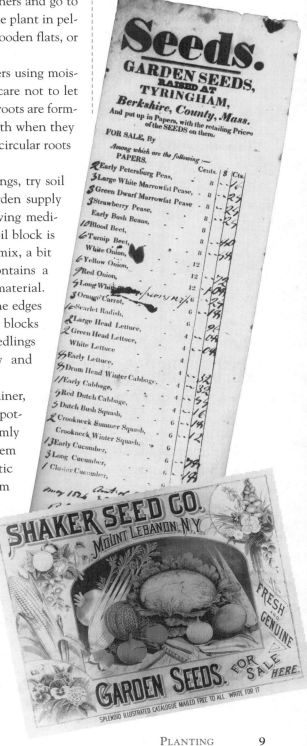

▶

Sod homes were a temporary
solution in treeless Nebraska;
for microbes, soil is the housing
of choice.

LIFE UNDERGROUND

Every day, millions of microbes lay down their lives for your garden.

In a single teaspoonful of good garden soil, there may be as many as five billion living organisms. As gardening editor Charlie Walters once noted, more forms of minute livestock are hidden in the soil than ever walk its surface, and their numbers are enormous. Even their weight, added together, is far heavier than that of all the humans, cows, horses, rabbits, mice, deer, toads, snakes, birds, insects, and other animals that move across the soil or burrow into it.

These minute organisms, microbes, came before everything else that lives on earth, including plants. The soil is their natural home, and they built it themselves. Tiny, toothless, and mouthless, they ingest through their membranes. In an ongoing chemical process, they chew up and digest the elements of bare, hard rock, laying down their lives and their bodies to produce life-sustaining humus.

It is the nature of microbes to recycle the elements of the soil through their bodies, creating a fertile environment for growing

There are more organisms in a single teaspoonful of good garden soil than there are sun worshipers at Coney Island on a hot summer's day.

plants. They turn nitrogen into nitrate, phosphorus into phosphate, sulfur into sulfate, chlorine into chloride, boron into borate, molybdenum into molybdate, and so on. They feed on both inorganic matter and organic compounds, gobbling up plant and animal tissues left in the soil, recycling dead cells. They attack sugars and cellulose first, as those are quick to decompose. When the sugars and cellulose are used up, most of the microbes die, contributing their carcasses to make up half of any soil's organic matter. (Microbes have short life spans, but they also procreate rapidly; a single microbe can produce 300 million descendants in a day.) The rest of the soil's components oxidize more slowly, helping humus to hold water. Without microbes to capture nitrogen from the air, all life forms would die from nitrogen starvation. But then, without microbes, those life forms would never have evolved in the first place.

All these little lives, reproductions, and deaths take place, of course, without any help from humans. The real work is done, largely without our knowledge, in the underground — while we do little more than scratch at the surface of the earth. ☀

The Peanut Butter Jar Soil Test

For those in a hurry, Wayne Cahilly, manager of the arboretum and grounds at The New York Botanical Garden, devised this simple yet sound 1-hour soil composition test.

Find a straight-sided jar. (A Mason jar or a peanut butter jar works well.) Slowly pour in a representative sample of your soil until the jar is between one-third and one-half full. Then fill it to the shoulder with water. Let the soil soak up water. Add 1 tablespoon Calgon, a surfactant that will break down the water's surface tension. Put the lid on the jar and shake the daylights out of it for 3 minutes. Set the jar down and look at your watch. In 1 minute, measure (with a ruler) the amount of sediment that has collected at the bottom. This is the sand in your soil.

Wait 4 minutes more. Measure the sediment again. The difference between the two numbers will be the amount of silt in your soil. Take a third measurement in 24 hours. The difference between the second and third numbers will be the amount of clay in the soil.

Now assume that the total is 100 percent. Calculate the percentages of sand, silt, and clay, which should add up to 100 percent. This test is simple but works well and can be helpful in deciding what to grow. You know that if your soil is high in sand, it will drain well. Silt and clay are hard to get wet, but they stay wet. Choose your plants accordingly.

He who sows thickly, gathers thinly.
He who sows thinly, gathers thickly.

— *OLD-TIME SAYING*

A SOWING LESSON

When it comes to sowing seeds, computer hackers have an advantage.

Seeds are remarkably persistent. They move by air, water, and animal hosts, attaching themselves by burrs and a variety of other mechanisms, often traveling great distances. They are tolerant of surprising abuse. Raspberry seeds have germinated after being boiled for jam, eaten, and digested. Tomato seeds endure gastric juices and pass smartly through the guts of animals; splendid crops of tomato plants are often seen growing in sewage works. Still, it helps if the gardener knows a few tricks.

The Tricks

☞ **Use a light hand**. Scatter seeds as if you were feeding chickens.

☞ **Get them in a little hot water.** Lupines, mallows, morning glories, okra, parsley, parsnips, and sweet peas need a good soaking to soften their hard seed coats before they are planted. Place them in six times their volume of hot (not boiling) water and let them soak for 24 hours. Or file them carefully with sandpaper or an emery board, or nick them gently with a knife.

☞ **Sometimes a little protection can help.** Start slow-sprouting seeds such as onions, parsley, and beets under a strip of burlap, which will warm the soil and let water in. Check them several times a day for signs of sprouting and remove the cover at the first sign of growth.

☞ **See how much they can take.** Put parsley seeds in the freezer for several days before planting, or soak them in boiling water.

☞ **Shake them up**. Mix fine seeds with coffee grounds, peat, vermiculite, or unflavored gelatin (which may give the seeds an extra boost of protein) and scatter them from a saltshaker.

☞ **Mix and match.** When planting a large yard or meadow, mix four parts sand to one part seeds before sowing. On a small lot, water the seeds in with a fan-type nozzle on the hose or watering can; when

Look to the Lilac Leaf

For generations, farmers have practiced what's known as phenology, from the Greek meaning the science of appearances. Simply put, phenology means watching natural indicators to know when it's safe to sow seed outdoors. Keep an eye on the lilac bushes, for example; experts advise that when their flowers are in full bloom, it's time to plant your beans. Like weather forecasting, phenology is largely a matter of experience. If the air and earth are warm in mid-May, and the apple trees are blossoming when the gardener sets out her garden, encountering no frosts, the next year she is likely to do the same — cued, perhaps, by the apple tree. Curious phenological lore abounds, and much of it is surprisingly accurate. For example, some folks say you should . . .

PLANT THESE CROPS	WHEN
Hardy crops	Peach and plum trees are in bloom
Corn	Elm leaves are the size of a squirrel's ear or oak leaves are the size of a mouse's ear or the dogwoods are in full bloom
Lettuce, peas, and spinach	Lilacs are in first leaf
Beans and squash	Lilacs are in full bloom
Perennials	Maples are coming into leaf

There's just one problem with this approach, as far as we can see: exactly how big *is* a mouse's ear?

the water hits the ground, the soil will bunch up and cover the seeds.

☞ **Space out.** Ensure even seed spacing by recycling the edges of perforated computer paper. Place the seeds in every hole or every third or fourth hole to get the spacing you need.

☞ **Wrap things up.** When planting hard-to-see seeds, roll out white toilet tissue, sow the seeds on it, cover them with another layer of tissue, wet the tissue, and cover the whole business with soil.

The Timing

☞ **Keep an eye on the forecast.** Sow perennial seeds outdoors up to 6 weeks before the first fall frost is expected. This gives young plants a chance to get going before a freeze, and they'll be ready to bloom the year after they're planted.

☞ **Place them in the deep freeze.** For the earliest blooms next spring and summer, plant seeds of hardy annuals such as alyssums, calendulas, calliopsis, cleomes, cosmos, pinks, portulacas, and zinnias outdoors just before the ground freezes. Place the seeds a bit deeper than you would in the spring and cover the beds with pine branches or boards to prevent them from washing away. ☀

THINK ABOUT IT

It is the quality of work that tells in the end, just as brainwork tells better than muscle. What is the use of a brain if we're not to use it? An ox can pull as well as a man, but he can't think as much. Let each one do what he can do best.

— *THE OLD FARMER'S ALMANAC, 1918*

Perfect Companions

When it comes to companion planting, nobody does it better than Native American gardeners, who for generations have planted beans, squash (or pumpkins), and corn together in the perfect symbiotic relationship. Native Americans call these plants the "Three Sisters of Life" — and as in any good family, each member supports the others. The cornstalks offer poles for the beans, which in turn supply nitrogen for the corn. The broad, spiny leaves of the squash vines, growing on the sides of the hills, provide mulch and deter predators. We'd be hard-pressed to improve on the arrangement.

Tips for Transplanting

Sowing is one thing; transplanting young seedlings is an equally tricky business with its own rules for success. Here are a few of them:

- **Handle with care.** This is the time to have a tender touch and all supplies at hand.

- **Choose your moment.** The best time to do it is on a misty or cloudy day or late in the afternoon when the sun is low.

- **Make contact.** Poke a hole in loose soil and press the roots firmly in contact with the soil.

- **Water sparingly.** Seedlings need moisture, of course, but don't overdo it.

- **Be protective.** Don't allow the seedlings to be damaged by strong winds or strong light. Shield the young plants from direct sunshine for a day or so, or provide them with a cloche or row cover to raise daytime temperatures and speed growth. (Remember, you are dealing with the very young.)

- **Be selective.** Transplant only young seedlings. At the beginning of the season, this may seem inevitable, but continued decisiveness on your part is crucial to the late-summer yield. For a beautiful crop of tender lettuce, for example, sow seeds every month and transplant them as soon as they are ready. Toss out seedlings that have been crowded in their beds, their development arrested; they are old and impotent.

- **Toughen them up.** Seedlings started indoors need a period of transition (about 2 weeks) before they are exposed to the outdoors. This process, known as hardening off, allows them to adjust to wind, direct sunlight, and fluctuating temperatures. On their first outings, plants need shelter and must come in for the night. Later, when they have toughened, they may stay out overnight in a sheltered spot.

- **Keep a warm spot for them — but not too warm.** Cold frames are good for hardening off, but never leave them closed on a warm day. Entire crops have been lost in a few hours when the temperature rose too high too fast.

WAIT TILL THE MOON IS FULL
At least if you're growing potatoes . . .

Romantics and scientists agree: the moon does have an effect on the affairs of men, although whether that effect is emotional or limited to the ebbing and flowing of the tides is still a subject of debate. And traditional gardeners hold that the moon also has an effect on your garden.

For centuries, it has been common to link planting times to the phases of the moon. Tradition has it that crops that grow underground — root crops such as potatoes, carrots, and beets — should be sown during the dark of the moon, from the day after the moon is full to the day before it is new again. Biodynamic gardeners explain that during this time, the plant orients itself toward the root, its sap rushing downward. (They reason that this is also a favorable time for transplanting.)

Crops that mature above the ground — leafy vegetables, grains, cabbage crops, parsley, peppers, and cucumbers — should be planted during the light of the moon, from the day the moon is new to the day it is full. During this period, the sap is said to flow upward more strongly, filling the plant with vitality.

Many gardeners plant potatoes right after the full moon, beans right after the change to the new moon. The last quarter, most moon planters say, is a barren time, best for weeding and cultivating.

Churchgoers point out that Easter is always the first Sunday after the first full moon of spring. Just two days before Easter is Good Friday, traditional potato-planting day in many places. Thus, potatoes planted on Good Friday will begin to settle into the soil during the dark of the moon.

If the gravitational pull of the moon raises ground water the way it does the ocean's tides, it makes sense that it may pull nutrients from a plant's roots to its leaves, thus stimulating growth. Some studies have shown that seeds do take in water and germinate according to a lunar cycle. Others have documented that certain flowering plants, such as sweet peas, need a period of total darkness to bloom.

If sweet peas start to set buds during the dark of the moon, it may be that the extreme blackness triggers the hormones that cause bloom. Budding during the full moon, then, would be delayed by the light.

Does lunar planting work? Try planting your potatoes after the full moon and see for yourself . . . . ☀

THREE WAYS TO HELP MOSS SPREAD

Relatively instant aging techniques for new rock gardens.

Some gardeners dislike moss; these are usually the people who work themselves into dementia or an early grave trying to achieve the "perfect" turf lawn. The fact is, though, that moss is beautiful when growing in its natural environment — preferably a cool, damp spot with acidic soil, one that receives shade or partial shade during the day. Cool, green moss also softens the look of landscape rocks or rock gardens, lending an air of noble antiquity.

All true mosses are bryophytes, nonflowering plants that branch out rather slowly on their own. To create the impression of an older garden, try some of these tricks — some ancient, some quite modern — to speed up the process and encourage moss to spread.

The Traditional Japanese Method

The Japanese are masters of rock gardening, and they keep their mossy rocks happy by sprinkling them with water in which they have rinsed rice. This rice water contains starches that nourish the moss.

The Big Rock Candy Mountain Method

If you have an area where moss would grow well naturally, bring in a moss-covered rock from a site that has similar conditions of light and moisture. Position the mossy rock near other rocks that are already in place and sprinkle the bare rocks with a sugar-water solution to encourage the moss to spread onto them. Keep the rocks slightly wet until the moss is established.

The High-Tech Kitchen Appliance Method

We recently heard of a gardener who had propagated moss by taking some existing moss from her back yard and putting it in a blender with some buttermilk (which has an acidity that moss likes). After processing the moss and milk into a kind of horticultural frappe, she sprinkled the mixture over a prepared bed and watered it lightly until the moss became established. ☀

When is a boulder not a rock?
Why, when it's a tea table for
upwardly mobile picnickers.

WHAT MAKES ROCKS RISE?

The push-me-pull-you theories of how all those rocks got into our gardens.

One of the givens of gardening in the North is the bumper crop of rocks that rises to the surface of the ground each spring. Most folks assume (quite correctly) that rocks rise on account of frost action in the ground. Yet only recently have scientists determined how freezing and thawing over the winter actually bring the stones to the surface.

Water expands when it freezes, and geologists have long postulated that this frozen moisture in the soil could move rocks to the surface in one of two ways — either by pushing the rocks up from below or by pulling them up from above.

The Push Theory assumes that freezing temperatures penetrate subsurface rocks faster than the soil surrounding them. This causes water underneath a rock to freeze (and expand) before water in the surrounding soil, pushing the rock upward. When the soil thaws in spring, the theory holds, a platform of ice supports the rock until soil can slip down into the cavity underneath. Result: The rock has moved up, staying roughly in the same place into which it was pushed by the frost.

The Pull Theory claims that soil freezes around the top of a rock first, grabbing it and pulling it upward as it heaves with frost.

From the looks of things, rocks grow even on the moon.

When this happens, loose, unfrozen soil around the base of the rock fills in the cavity underneath. Result: Same as the Push Theory — a rocky soil and a lot of work for discouraged gardeners.

A few years ago, researcher Suzanne Prestrud Anderson of the University of Washington set out to solve this push-me-pull-you controversy once and for all. She embedded several heat-sensitive metal rods into a chunk of gneiss (a granitelike rock) and buried the stone in a wastebasket-size container filled with silty soil. Over the next 4 months, she put the container through seven cycles of freezing and thawing in a cold chamber. Result: The Pull Theory won. The rock heaved upward after the soil around its top had frozen. In fact, in the course of her experiment, it rose a full 5 inches, breaking through the surface of the soil.

Unfortunately, this scientific breakthrough offers little practical benefit to gardeners. Every year we pick out the new crop of stones before planting, assuming that someday the earth will simply run out of raw material. (It never will.) About the only thing we can do to reduce rocks is to build up our soil over a period of years, adding organic matter to encourage soil life and make it loose and fertile even deep below the surface. This technique may not eliminate all upwardly mobile rocks, but your plants will love you (and that may make you more philosophical about any stones you do find). ☀

When Is It Time to Plant?

Some folks plant by the appropriate phases of the moon; others practice phenology. An eighty-year-old farmer we know has a different technique. "I just wait until I see the weeds starting to grow in my garden," he told us. "Then I know it's time to plant." If none of those tests seems right for you, try one of these.

THE FOOTPRINT TEST

Step into the garden and then stand back and look at the footprint you've left. If it's shiny, there's too much water near the soil's surface to dig and plant. If it's dull, excess water has drained away, and it's time to plant.

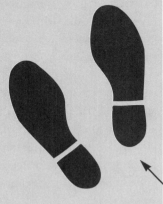

THE HANDFUL TEST

Take up a handful of garden soil and squeeze it into a ball, then drop it. If it shatters or crumbles, it's ready for seeds; if it holds its shape or breaks into two clumps, it's still too wet.

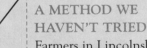

A METHOD WE HAVEN'T TRIED

Farmers in Lincolnshire, England, once practiced a unique custom for determining planting time. They took off their trousers and sat on the earth; if it was warm and comfortable enough for them, they reasoned, it would be comfortable for their plants.

PLANTS THAT COVER A LOT OF GROUND

If mowing the lawn (again) is not your idea of a great weekend morning, read on.

Americans spend $5 billion a year coddling the carpet that covers 30 million acres of our soil.

▼

For anyone who hates mowing the lawn, a simple solution is at hand: don't plant your lawn in grass. An alternative to the indentured servitude required by grass is to plant a ground cover on your lawn instead. Ground covers represent a large group of plants, ones that are every bit as attractive as turf grass but that grow happily by themselves, requiring little or no maintenance. Some even grow vigorously in areas where grass does poorly — on a steep, dry slope that's impossible to mow, or in a wet, shady spot under tall trees. Better yet, there's a ground cover that's perfectly suited to almost any location or any taste.

What's more, many ground covers are actually more attractive than a turf lawn during certain seasons. Some are evergreens, while others sport brightly colored flowers in the spring or summer or spectacular foliage and berries in the fall. Still others are sweet-smelling herbs like chamomile, which seems to grow better the more you step on it.

Some ground covers spread like wildfire, and once they become established, you may need to weed them out periodically to keep them within bounds. To save yourself

time, plant them where they can spread to their heart's content. The only other maintenance you may need to perform is to water them occasionally during hot, dry weather and to run over them with the mower once or twice a year (a lot less work than mowing grass every week).

In fact, selecting your favorite ground cover from among all the plants available will probably prove to be more work than caring for it. Following are our top picks for beautiful, low-care plants.

Bearberry (*Arctostaphylos Uva-ursi*). Evergreen; red fruit; good for planting on steep banks.

Carpet bugleweed (*Ajuga reptans*). Beautiful blue-purple flowers; spreads rapidly; does well in either sun or shade.

Creeping juniper (*Juniperus horizontalis*). Evergreen; blue fruit; grows well on steep banks and in any kind of soil.

English ivy (*Hedera helix*). Evergreen; good on steep banks; does well in either sun or shade; spreads quickly; grows well in any kind of soil.

Forget-me-not (*Myosotis scorpioides*). Beautiful blue flowers with white, pink, or yellow centers; withstands shade and thrives in wet soils.

Lily of the valley (*Convallaria majalis*). Spreads quickly; bell-shaped white or rose flowers have wonderful fragrance; orange fruit; grows well in shade and in any kind of soil.

Oregon holly grape (*Mahonia Aquifolium*). Evergreen; shiny dark green leaves turn bronze in fall; showy yellow flowers and blue-black fruit; grows well in either sun or shade and in any kind of soil.

Ribbon grass (*Phalaris arundinacea picta*). Name comes from the pretty variegated white-and-green blades; spreads rapidly; good for steep banks; grows well in dry and wet soils and in either sun or shade.

Virginia creeper (*Parthenocissus quinquefolia*). Rapidly growing vine with five-lobed leaves that turn bright yellow to red in fall; blue-black fruit; good choice for steep, sunny banks.

Not Available at Your Average Garden Store...

We normally think of seeds as tiny sparks of life, ready to sprout and grow almost miraculously given the right conditions. As the old saying goes, "Tall oaks from little acorns grow." Yet in reality, seeds come in all shapes and sizes, and many would never fit into the little paper packets that you buy at the nursery or receive through the mail.

The largest known seed on earth belongs to the koco-de-mer, or double coconut (*Lodoicea maldivica*), a native of the Seychelles in the Indian Ocean. The name *double coconut* derives from the fact that the huge seeds have two distinct lobes divided by a central cleft. The koco-de-mer requires 10 years from the time of flowering to ripen its seeds, and individual specimens can reach 18 inches in length and weigh up to 40 pounds.

By contrast, the smallest seeds in the world are produced by certain epiphytic (air-dwelling) orchids. According to *The Guinness Book of Records*, it takes 35 million orchid seeds to make 1 ounce.

Elizabeth Tashjian, of the Nut Museum in Old Lyme, Connecticut, with a single seed of the koco-de-mer.

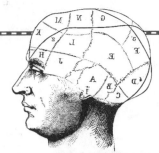

TEST YOUR PLANTING KNOWLEDGE

1 It's the middle of winter, and you're going through your collection of old seeds. There you find a few partial packets of vegetable seeds left over from last year, and you wonder whether they're still viable. Assuming that the seeds were viable last year and that you've stored them properly, which of the following common vegetable seeds would be *least* likely to germinate well this year?

   a. onions
   b. turnips
   c. carrots
   d. beans

2 The seeds of certain trees and bushes require special treatment before planting. In nature, these seeds would normally drop from their parent plants and winter over in the cold, wet ground. Gardeners mimic nature by wintering the seeds over in the refrigerator or in a container of cool, moist sand or peat moss. What is the name of this procedure?

   a. acclimatization
   b. cold germination
   c. stratification
   d. scarification

3 We often assume that seeds require a covering of earth — however thin — at planting time. Yet many kinds of flower seeds actually need light to germinate and should not be covered with earth. Which of the following common flower seeds requires exposure to light?

   a. petunia
   b. snapdragon
   c. impatiens
   d. all of the above

ANSWERS

1. a. If properly stored in a sealed bag in a cool, dry place, most vegetable seeds remain viable for at least 3 years (some, like beans and melons, for 5 years). Onions are one of the few exceptions, losing much of their viability after 1 year. Other short-lived seeds include sweet corn, beets, parsnips, and salsify.
2. c. The purpose of stratification is to soften the seed's hard coat and give it the period of cooling it needs before it is planted in the spring. *Scarification,* on the other hand, involves nicking the hard coat of a seed (like spinach) with a file before planting to speed germination.
3. d.

CHAPTER TWO

THE WEATHER & YOUR GARDEN

"THERE ARE A NUMBER OF TRICKS FOR DECEIVING THE WEATHER AND MAKING IT CHANGE. IF FOR INSTANCE, I DECIDE TO PUT ON THE WARMEST CLOTHES I POSSESS, THE TEMPERATURE USUALLY RISES. AND A THAW ALSO SETS IN IF SOME FRIENDS ARRANGE TO GO TO THE MOUNTAINS TO SKI. . . .

"IF IT WERE OF ANY USE, EVERY DAY THE GARDENER WOULD FALL ON HIS KNEES AND PRAY SOMEHOW LIKE THIS: 'O LORD, GRANT THAT IN SOME WAY IT MAY RAIN EVERY DAY, SAY FROM ABOUT MIDNIGHT UNTIL THREE O'CLOCK IN THE MORNING, BUT YOU SEE, IT MUST BE GENTLE AND WARM SO THAT IT CAN SOAK IN; GRANT THAT AT THE SAME TIME IT WOULD NOT RAIN ON CAMPION, ALYSSUM, HELIANTHEMUM, LAVENDER, AND THE OTHERS WHICH YOU IN YOUR INFINITE WISDOM KNOW ARE DROUGHT-LOVING PLANTS — I WILL WRITE THEIR NAMES ON A BIT OF PAPER IF YOU LIKE — AND GRANT THAT THE SUN MAY SHINE THE WHOLE DAY LONG, BUT NOT EVERYWHERE . . . AND NOT TOO MUCH; THAT THERE MAY BE PLENTY OF DEW AND LITTLE WIND, ENOUGH WORMS, NO PLANT-LICE AND SNAILS, NO MILDEW, AND THAT ONCE A WEEK THIN LIQUID MANURE AND GUANO MAY FALL FROM HEAVEN. AMEN.' FOR SO IT WAS IN THE GARDEN OF EDEN; OTHERWISE THINGS WOULD NOT HAVE GROWN IN IT AS WELL AS THEY DID."

— KAREL CAPEK, *THE GARDENER'S YEAR*

"LOOKS LIKE RAIN"

Old-time tricks that still work today.

Old-timers knew the weather better than we do, probably because they were closer to it, unprotected by storm windows, air conditioners, and central heating. There were sailors, farmers, and woodsmen who could glance at an afternoon sky and guess right three times out of four about the next day's weather. They were weather-wise almost by instinct; they had weather sense. They had only to observe certain cloud formations in specific months when the wind was thus and the temperature so; by the unconscious recollection of similar conditions, they could determine what was likely to be.

Scientific weather forecasting has come a long way, yet it has never completely supplanted the observation of plants, animals, and insects. There are probably more folk sayings connected with the weather than with any other subject — reflecting both a direct link to our agricultural heritage and our continuing instinctive concern for our fields, our gardens, our food sources, our dinners, our well-being, and our lives.

The traditional weather indicators still have real value today, often demonstrating in a down-to-earth, readily identifiable way the same phenomena that the meteorologists follow. We know, for example, that the temperature of the air increases and the dew point rises just before a rainstorm. But a traditional Native American saying puts it far more directly: "When the locks turn damp in the scalp house, surely it will rain."

THE BIRDS KNOW

WHEN THE BIRDS NEST LOW,
ALL THE YEAR THE WINDS
WILL BLOW.

— OLD WEATHER PROVERB

Just Thinking

When the gardener complains about the weather, he is always on firm ground. There is always good reason for complaint; nothing is reliable, and outrageous weather is not only natural but inevitable.

If you don't have a scalp house nearby, keep an eye out for these other traditional signs of rain.

Plants

Aspen trees	Turn up their leaves
Flowers (all kinds)	Give off a stronger scent than usual
Milkweed	Closes
Mushrooms	Sprout
Pitcher plants	Open up

Animals

Bees	Head for the hive
Cows	Become restless and stretch their necks
Dogs	Burrow into the dirt
Fish	Swim near the surface and bite readily
Flies	Bite
Fowl	Roll in the dust or sand
Horses	Sweat in the stable
Parrots	Whistle
Roosters	Crow at evening
Sheep	Collect in a flock
Snakes	Expose themselves
Spiders	Reinforce their webs
Swallows	Circle and call, or graze the ground
Trout	Jump

KEEP ON KEEPING ON

- - - - - - - - - - - - - - -

"What of a drought?" says a voice. We answer, we keep doing and trust in Providence. Yes, we keep doing.

— THE OLD FARMER'S ALMANAC, 1850

MISS OHIO   MISS ILLINOIS   MISS KANSAS   MISS PENNSYLVANIA

▶ If you know cows, you know they know when rain's on the way.

And All the Rest

Bread and cheese..Soften
Dishes...Sweat
Ditches..Stink
Ropes...Shorten and twist
Salt ....Forms cakes
Stars ....Sparkle more brightly than usual
Tobacco...Becomes moist

A sign of rain: Tobacco becomes moist.

▼

HOW SOON WE FORGET

THERE IS NO POINT
DREADING THE NEXT
SUMMER STORM THAT . . .
WILL FLATTEN EVERYTHING.
NOR IS THERE ANY POINT
DREADING THE WINTER, SO
SOON TO COME, IN WHICH
THE TEMPERATURES WILL
DROP TO TEN BELOW ZERO
AND THE GROUND FREEZES
FORTY INCHES DEEP AND WE
ALL SAY THERE NEVER WAS
SUCH A WINTER SINCE THE
BEGINNING OF THE WORLD.
THERE HAVE BEEN SUCH
WINTERS; THERE WILL
BE MORE.

— HENRY MITCHELL,
THE ESSENTIAL EARTHMAN

"Gonna Be a Tough Winter"

Few things concern the gardener more than the first warning signs of winter, and few events are greater cause for chagrin than the onset of an unexpected frost. But those who believe in keeping a close eye on nature will find portents aplenty for predicting just how harsh the upcoming winter will be. The following are all considered traditional signs of a severe winter ahead:

Bears	Are seen berrying
Chipmunks	Are abundant
Geese	Fly south at a high altitude
Lakes and rivers	Freeze later than usual
Onions	Grow thicker skins than usual
Squirrels	Are scarce
Woodpeckers	Appear early

When it comes to long-range weather forecasting, sometimes nature can be more accurate than the local meteorologist. So the next time a friend tells you to be sure to protect your garden against an especially harsh winter ahead, ask him if he's checked his onions lately.

Cloudy Visions

Meteorologists have identified more than a hundred types of clouds, but for practical purposes, English scientist Luke Howard's classification, from the early nineteenth century, will do.

1 Cumulus. Also called cauliflower clouds, these are the white, fluffy heads of rising columns of air. Old-timers said, "If woolly fleeces spread the heavenly way, be sure no rain disturbs the summer's day." But this prophecy applies only as long as the clouds remain white and horizontal, like sheep's fleece. When these formations turn to the dark cumulonimbus variety (also known as thunderclouds), watch for rain.

2 Stratus. A low layer of flat, sheetlike gray clouds, created by the general rise of a layer of air. "Yellow streaks in sunset sky," the old proverb says, "wind and daylong rain are nigh."

3 Cirrus. These curly, lacy clouds, composed entirely of ice crystals, form high in the sky, created by whirls or eddies in the air. They're often described as "feathery" and reminiscent of mares' tails. As long as the tails point downward, fair weather is likely to lie ahead. But when the tails turn upward, rain is likely.

MAP OUT YOUR MICROCLIMATES

Without this personal weather map, you are doomed to distress.

A microclimate is a relatively small area within a climatic zone, a
neighborhood, or even an individual garden that has a different
climate than its surroundings. When you plan your garden, you'd
be well advised to examine the microclimates there and to keep
these general rules in mind.

Where the Ground Is Elevated, the Temperature's Not

☞ Temperature is much influenced by elevation. In general, the higher the elevation, the colder the air is.

☞ The direction in which a slope faces is also a factor. South-facing hillsides collect warmth; north-facing hillsides are cooler.

☞ Indentations in slopes let cold air drain off, as hollows, hedges, and walls hold it.

Wall Flowers Have Special Concerns

☞ Walls, buildings, walkways, and even bushes hold heat in summer and cold in winter. Sections thus bordered will have more extreme climates than adjacent areas of the garden.

☞ Siting tender plants near the side of a building facing east shelters them from prevailing winter winds and provides them with some stored heat.

NICE WEATHER FOR LETTUCE

WEATHER MEANS MORE WHEN YOU HAVE A GARDEN. THERE'S NOTHING LIKE LISTENING TO A SHOWER AND THINKING HOW IT IS SOAKING IN AND AROUND YOUR LETTUCE AND GREEN BEANS.

— HENRY VAN DYKE

If the gardener's footstep is fine fertilizer, how much finer the footfalls of a whole flock of tiny feet?

Watch Out for Wind Tunnels

☞ A solid wall can retain the sun's heat and promote plant growth, but it doesn't work well as a windbreak. Like trees and buildings, solid walls can act as funnels for prevailing winds.

☞ Open hedges and fences can weaken a wind's strength. Plan your landscape accordingly.

Avoid Jack Frost Nipping at Your Rows

☞ Low-lying areas are subject to frost.

☞ Open spaces also are likely to attract frost because they allow the day's heat to be radiated up to the open sky and absorbed by the atmosphere.

☞ If a frost is rolling through a north-facing field, the north side of a house — or any other obstruction — will trap and hold it. Cold, like water, runs downhill and pools in hollows.

Give Your Plants an Oceanfront View

☞ Nearness to the ocean or a large body of water not only increases the supply of moisture but also moderates temperature — making the area warmer in winter and cooler in summer. Land even a few miles from a river is less temperate than that in the river valley.

These general principles are a beginning, but the best measures of your garden's microclimates are trial and error, observation and reaction. If a plant doesn't thrive in one spot, move it —it may do much better in another. As there is probably an ideal temperature for every plant, and for every stage in its maturation process, there is probably a site best suited for its growth and development as well. All you have to do is find it. ☀

◀ Never underestimate the power of a stiff breeze.

Nature's Plow

SOMETHING THERE IS THAT DOESN'T LOVE A WALL,

THAT SENDS THE FROZEN-GROUND-SWELL UNDER IT,

AND SPILLS THE UPPER BOULDERS IN THE SUN,

AND MAKES GAPS EVEN TWO CAN PASS ABREAST.

— ROBERT FROST

Frost is nature's plow, and gardeners who consider it an enemy should think again. Frost is a mighty mill, capable of cracking boulders and leveling huge landmasses — after all, it was the accumulation of frost and ice in the last great Ice Age that rearranged our ranges and ridges, lakes and rivers. All our precious topsoil, host to every plant on the planet, has provided life and sustenance thanks to the millions of tons of ground-up rock dust milled by melting glaciers and spread over the face of the earth by wind and rain. It's a slow process, to be sure, gradual but continuous, that has covered the earth with a rind of soil like the rind of an orange, if far less uniform.

People need a power drill or a blast of dynamite to do what a drop of frozen water can do. Confronted with a huge rock, a drop of water can roll into a hollow or slip into a crevice even a root couldn't penetrate, then wait for cold. When the freezing spell arrives, the water expands in turning to ice and the rock breaks apart, loosened in its bed, changing the very shape of the hillside.

Even in the space of a garden's life, frost helps to till and improve the soil, breaking rocks into finer and finer particles until their minerals become usable by plants. Frost is an immense, omnipotent plow that does the heavy work, shaking the stubble of the corn fields; destroying germs and pests; and, with the help of earthworms, breaking up, stirring, and loosening hard-packed soil. The whole crust of the land crackles and crumbles, lifted from the subsoil on a million tiny needles of ice, raised up and stirred and opened to the air.

HAVE YOU TRIED HOT-WIRING YOUR TOMATOES?
Dedicated gardeners will go to almost any lengths to outwit the weather. For instance . . .

Gardeners often go to extremes to avoid the heart-break of a killing frost; sometimes this may call for a pact with the devil himself.

Certain gardeners grow the impossible. Plants that shouldn't even survive in their climates flourish in their gardens. Why? In general, their successes are accomplishments, not accidents, and the results of canny planning as well as trial and error.

A Connecticut gardener we know manages to grow tender camellias in his northern climate by focusing on the bywords familiar to real estate

agents everywhere: location, location, location. He sets the plants near the foundation on the north side of his house. Choosing the coldest spot means that the ground is less likely to thaw in winter and spares the camellias the desiccating thawing and refreezing that is so stressful to plants. (Stress-free plants, like stress-free people, seem to be healthier and live longer.)

The Connecticut gardener has managed to outwit the weather in a logical, straightforward way. Others go to greater extremes. A gardener challenged by the weather, it seems, is sometimes a gardener possessed.

☞ Have you heard the one about the Georgia gardener who stood over her tomatoes with an umbrella for the duration of a hailstorm?

☞ How about the cricket-dung aficionado from upstate New York who gets his designer mulch delivered overnight by Federal Express?

☞ Then there's the Ontario gardener who's so determined to pick early tomatoes that he sinks an electric heating unit into the soil under his seedlings, as well as a 1½-inch plastic pipe packed in peat moss, to treat the lower root system with warm water.

☞ A Fairbanks, Alaska, man on the same wavelength runs pipes from his hot-water heater outside and under his vegetable bed, then back indoors.

☞ Another Alaska gardener buries Styrofoam under his corn patch to hold heat and block frost.

☞ A San Antonio man overwinters bananas in his back yard by cutting the main trunks back to about 8 feet in late fall, removing all the leaves, and wrapping the trunks loosely in heavy clear plastic.

☞ Deep South gardeners challenged by extremes of heat and drought go to great lengths to grow cool-climate crops. One southern vegetable gardener keeps his lettuce heads cool with raised row covers

GROWLY SKIES

The sky begins to look growly, and if you are not prepared for a boxing-match with a northeaster, you had better be picking up your tools, that you may be ready for the encounter.

— THE OLD FARMER'S ALMANAC, 1850

EYES OPEN!

If we would train our eyes and
educate our minds so as to better
understand the wonderful book of
Nature, we should more fully realize the ever-presence of a
Supreme Ruler, and, in our ram-
bles over the fields, every step
would bring to our view objects of
the deepest interest.

— THE OLD FARMER'S ALMANAC, 1891

of cheesecloth on a wire frame, then sets a sprinkler to apply just enough water to match the evaporation rate but not wet the soil.

☞ A Florida gardener plants in recessed, rather than raised, beds — sunk about 6 inches so that water drains into them through the sandy soil and compost and mulch and seedlings don't drain out.

In gardening circles, it's become almost routine to hear stories of seeds left in the freezer for stratification, boiling water poured into the garden to hasten germination, gardening by moonlight (or headlights) on crucial spring nights, and all sorts of heroic late-summer efforts to fight frost. Committed tillers use row covers and cloches (made of materials ranging from plastic, glass, wood, paper, and fabric to space-age synthetics), special cultivars, hardening techniques, and hastening techniques to enhance their yields. In short, gardeners enlist all the tricks of the trade to outwit the weather, simulate ideal growing conditions, and gain their horticultural ends.

The things we do for love! ☀

Poor Man's Fertilizer

UNDER THE SNOW THE VEGETABLES PURR

LIKE AN OLD MAN 'NEATH A MANTLE OF FUR.

— OLD SAYING

Old-timers knew that a spring snowfall ("poor man's fertilizer") was good for the garden, for like lightning, snow passing through the atmosphere picks up oxygen and nitrogen and delivers it to the soil. Yankee farmers took advantage of the phenomenon by plowing these light snows under — which, we figure, is how the phenomenon was first observed.

During a fierce and freakish blizzard in May 1891, corn was reported to have germinated and grown to a height of 3 inches beneath the snow. The ground was warm when the snow fell, and the snow had an insulating effect against the cold air above, for snow is a natural blanket. Without snow's protection, seeds of annuals and roots of perennials would freeze to death during the winter. In extremely cold weather, the temperature of the ground beneath a blanket of snow may be up to 50 degrees warmer than the air above.

That's why another old farmer's adage says, "A good winter with snow makes all the plants grow."

Much Ado About Mulches

Most gardeners are mad for mulch, and for good reason. After all, mulch — that is, any material applied to the surface of the soil to conserve moisture, moderate temperature, discourage weeds, prevent erosion, and maintain the physical structure of the soil — is a gardener's best ally against the destructive forces of weather. When the notion of covering gardens with organic material first came on the national gardening scene, it was earth shattering to Yankees who had always kept their plots under control in neat, pencil-straight rows. But even cautious New Englanders soon learned how effective — and easy — this simple technique can be. Gardeners started out mulching with straw or marsh hay, but experimentation led to diversification. Today, some use leaves (shredded or not), pine needles, wood chips, sawdust, bits of bark, pebbles, peanut shells, buckwheat hulls, cocoa husks (which have a wonderful chocolaty smell after a rain), newspapers, or what have you. Some urge, "Mulch your garden with living plants!"

The best mulch for your garden is one that's readily available, inexpensive, easy to apply, and — preferably — fit to look at. Not much to ask of a mulch!

An abundance of available mulch has moved many a man to merriment.

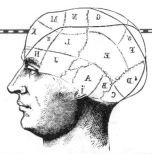

TEST YOUR WEATHER WISDOM

2 True or false: Clover can be used to predict approaching rain.

1 What kind of day is the best for establishing spring transplants in the garden?

a. sunny and hot
b. partly cloudy and breezy
c. humid and drizzly
d. any of the above

3 Which of the following vegetables is the least tolerant of cool temperatures?

a. radishes
b. okra
c. collards
d. parsnips
e. leeks

CHAPTER THREE

GARDEN DESIGN & TECHNIQUE

"THE HISTORY OF GARDEN DESIGN IS LIKE A TAPESTRY THAT COVERS EVERY CULTURE FROM EARLY CIVILIZATIONS TO THE PRESENT TIME. THE FABRIC IS THE PRODUCT OF MANY INFLUENCES: NATURAL FEATURES, RELIGIOUS BELIEFS, PHILOSOPHICAL THEORIES, SCIENTIFIC AND TECHNOLOGICAL ADVANCES, AND THE DESIRE TO IMPROVE ONE'S IMMEDIATE ENVIRONMENT, MAKING IT MORE PLEASANT AND PRODUCTIVE AND PRACTICAL.

"THROUGHOUT HISTORY, THE COMPONENTS OF GARDENS (PLANTS THAT FLOWER AND BEAR FRUIT, SHADE FOR PROTECTION FROM THE ELEMENTS, WATER THAT COOLS THE ATMOSPHERE AND IRRIGATES THE LAND, MAN-MADE OBJECTS FOR DELIGHT AND INTEREST) REMAIN CONSTANT, REGARDLESS OF THE GREAT VARIETY OF NATURAL PHENOMENA (GEOGRAPHY, CLIMATE, PLANT MATERIAL, TOPOGRAPHY) AND CULTURAL INFLUENCES (RELIGION, ARCHITECTURAL THEORIES, FUNCTIONAL DETERMINANTS) THAT MAKE GARDENS DIFFERENT. TO STUDY THESE DIFFERENCES IS TO FOLLOW THE PROGRESS OF GARDEN DESIGN. TO UNDERSTAND THESE DIFFERENCES IS TO GAIN AN APPRECIATION FOR HOW MAN HAS ALTERED — AND BEEN ALTERED BY — HIS PHYSICAL SURROUNDINGS."

—WILLIAM LAKE DOUGLAS, *A GARDEN PROGRESS*

AMERICA'S FIRST GARDEN

In the grounds around the White House, our nation's presidents have planted many clues to their personalities.

Considering our national predilection to train all eyes and cameras on every First Family foible, it's surprising how little Americans — even American gardeners — know about the grounds and gardens of the White House in Washington, D.C. This is unfortunate, because the White House gardens display both a legacy of presidential green thumbs and a history of trends in American garden design.

George Washington himself chose the site for the proposed White House and its gardens, originally called President's Park. In 1791,

Fleecy lawn mowers replaced groundskeepers on the White House lawns during Woodrow Wilson's administration, freeing the men to fight the War to End All Wars.

Abigail Adams described the area as a wilderness dotted with occasional clearings, and Pennsylvania Avenue as a muddy wagon track. Livestock roamed at large on the unfenced grounds where the White House would later stand, while squatters toasted squirrels over fires.

The earliest days of the park's development were trouble-ridden. Washington chose Pierre Charles L'Enfant to design America's new capital city, but the temperamental Frenchman couldn't get along with anyone else and was replaced by James Hoban, whose design for the White House is the one we know today. Hoban, as it happened, owned a small cottage on the very site, which he rented to a carpenter's wife during the construction. When she opened a brothel there, however, the development commission objected, the entrepreneur was fined, and the cottage was torn down.

John Adams was the first president to live in the White House, moving into the still unfinished building in November 1800. After Thomas Jefferson took over the following March, it's not surprising that the new president became personally involved in the development of the grounds. It was Jefferson who divided the grounds into two sectors: the northern was for public use and the southern, overlooking the Potomac, was for private First Family use. Collaborating with Benjamin Latrobe, he planted white pine, mountain ash, holly, and hemlock trees to screen and soften the lines of the house on all sides. For the future, Jefferson proposed a large garden area to the southeast for both ornamental and edible plants, arranged in parterres in the French manner.

BOUNTEOUS BORDERS

Borders for flowers should never be made too narrow. Five or six feet is a good width, while eight feet is better. Beds two to three feet wide suffer in dry weather and give less opportunity for grouping plants. One bed six feet wide is much better than two three feet wide.

Blank spaces occur in flower borders when bulbs like tulips and narcissus die down, or after such plants as lungwort and oriental poppies have lost their foliage. Sow seeds of poppies, calendula, and sweet alyssum in April when the bulbous plants are just coming up, and have a reserve bed of seedlings like zinnias or marigolds which can easily be transplanted into the vacant spaces. Bedding plants such as heliotrope, salvia, or rose geranium can also be used for this purpose.

— THE OLD FARMER'S ALMANAC, 1914

The next president, James Madison, executed that plan for the garden, as well as Jefferson's idea of planting specimen trees ranging from willow oaks to sugar maples to elms and horse chestnuts. The results of these efforts were largely lost, however, during the British invasion of 1814. Dolley Madison is remembered for valiantly saving George Washington's portrait from the burning White House, but even she couldn't save the gardens. James Madison's successor, James Monroe, had to replant virtually the entire 60 acres. *His* successor, John Quincy Adams, initiated a collection of American plants in the main ornamental garden and planted an American elm that stood on the South Lawn until 1991.

After the British, the next major assault on the White House gardens came not from a foreign power but from ordinary Americans. During the melee following Andrew Jackson's 1829 inauguration, the new president's enthusiastic supporters managed to trample much of the collection that Adams had so carefully installed. But Jackson made up for a bad beginning; during his second term, he went on a planting extravaganza. Jackson hired competent gardeners, who installed many new plants, including horse chestnuts, sycamores, elms, maples, and magnolias. An arbor was built, along with trellises and an orangery. A new 2-acre garden of roses and other flowers gave the President's Park a fashionable look at last.

Under Jackson, the city of Washington itself made a transition. The mall was paved, and the city was no longer a frontier town. The country was becoming civilized, and with it, the First Garden.

President Martin Van Buren, whose term followed, took constant flak for his extravagance and his salary ($25,000 a year). He was a sitting duck for bombast about appropriations for garden maintenance, even though most of the money had been spent by Jackson, man of the people. Still, by the end of Van Buren's term, Jefferson's overall design had been implemented. Shrubs were grouped, which made them convenient to water and to fence against wandering sheep and horses. The trees were attaining stature, and flowers, particularly roses, made beautiful focal points. All

THE PRESIDENT'S PARK: *This drawing is based on an aerial photograph and on a plan drawn by the National Park Service. Numbered trees and gardens are associated with Presidents or First Ladies. The key at right identifies trees planted by President and Mrs. Clinton and others by the name of the President in office when they were planted.*

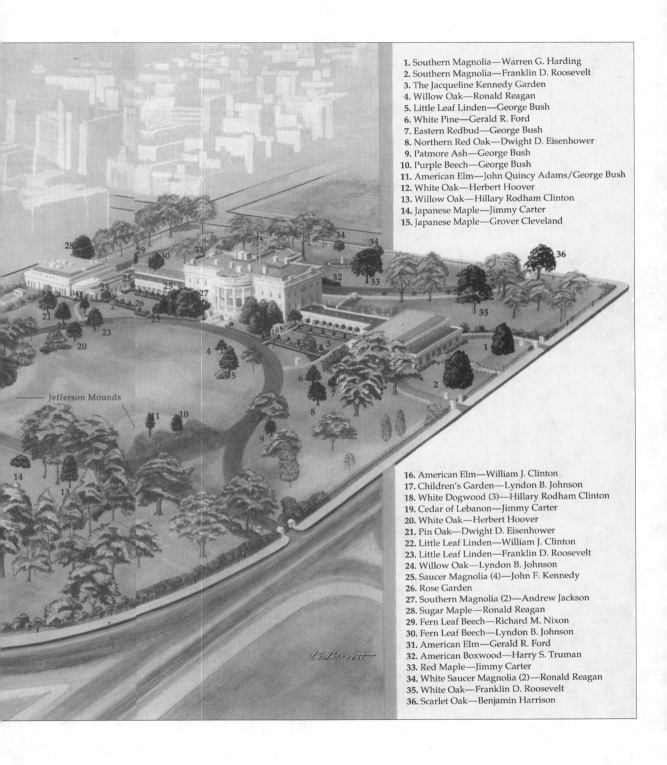

1. Southern Magnolia—Warren G. Harding
2. Southern Magnolia—Franklin D. Roosevelt
3. The Jacqueline Kennedy Garden
4. Willow Oak—Ronald Reagan
5. Little Leaf Linden—George Bush
6. White Pine—Gerald R. Ford
7. Eastern Redbud—George Bush
8. Northern Red Oak—Dwight D. Eisenhower
9. Patmore Ash—George Bush
10. Purple Beech—George Bush
11. American Elm—John Quincy Adams/George Bush
12. White Oak—Herbert Hoover
13. Willow Oak—Hillary Rodham Clinton
14. Japanese Maple—Jimmy Carter
15. Japanese Maple—Grover Cleveland

—Jefferson Mounds

16. American Elm—William J. Clinton
17. Children's Garden—Lyndon B. Johnson
18. White Dogwood (3)—Hillary Rodham Clinton
19. Cedar of Lebanon—Jimmy Carter
20. White Oak—Herbert Hoover
21. Pin Oak—Dwight D. Eisenhower
22. Little Leaf Linden—William J. Clinton
23. Little Leaf Linden—Franklin D. Roosevelt
24. Willow Oak—Lyndon B. Johnson
25. Saucer Magnolia (4)—John F. Kennedy
26. Rose Garden
27. Southern Magnolia (2)—Andrew Jackson
28. Sugar Maple—Ronald Reagan
29. Fern Leaf Beech—Richard M. Nixon
30. Fern Leaf Beech—Lyndon B. Johnson
31. American Elm—Gerald R. Ford
32. American Boxwood—Harry S. Truman
33. Red Maple—Jimmy Carter
34. White Saucer Magnolia (2)—Ronald Reagan
35. White Oak—Franklin D. Roosevelt
36. Scarlet Oak—Benjamin Harrison

this would last about 10 years — until it was ripped out by the next landscaper to tackle the First Garden.

Andrew Jackson Downing — author, landscape gardener, architect, and editor of *The Horticulturist* — worked under the approving eyes of Millard Fillmore. Downing redesigned the First Garden in the popular English romantic style, ripping out the earlier formal landscapes. He made complex, grandiose designs, fired men who had worked on the gardens all their lives, hired new workers, and cut down trees to make way for a statue of Andrew Jackson. In the end, however, most of Downing's plans went unrealized — interrupted by his own untimely death in a steamboat explosion, Fillmore's truncated career, and the tragedy of approaching civil war.

Franklin Pierce, the next occupant of the White House, was a Yankee with simple tastes. Pierce built a neat white picket fence around the private presidential flower garden. He also installed greenhouses (the first of several at the White House) filled with flowers and foliage and heated with a big coal-burning furnace.

Greenhouses became conservatories and were a large part of presidential private life until Theodore Roosevelt moved into the White House nearly half a century later. Roosevelt had the greenhouses and conservatories demolished and removed all the intricate flower beds from the front lawn.

After that, it was largely a game of horticultural musical chairs, continuing right up until Franklin Delano Roosevelt called in the illustrious landscape architect Frederick Law Olmsted. Olmsted's plans returned to many of Jefferson's ideas: he retained the thick stands of trees and shrubs bordering the lawns, installed an oval drive on the south side, and replaced the iron fences around the grounds. Flower beds near the east and west wings evolved into the two major gardens at the White House today.

According to Irvin Williams, current superintendent of White House grounds, things aren't likely to change much anytime soon. "The Olmsted plan is our Bible, so to speak," Williams says. John F. Kennedy's friend Bunny Mellon did redesign the West Garden, now the famous Rose Garden, where ceremonial functions are held, and also worked with Jacqueline Kennedy and Lady Bird Johnson in the East Garden, now known as the First Lady's Garden. Both areas have wide flower beds,

▲
Frederick Law Olmsted, a.k.a. the Father of Landscape Gardening.

◄
First Lady Lucy Webb Hayes poses in the White House conservatory in 1879 with (left to right) Fanny and Scott Hayes and Carrie Paulding Davis. Mrs. Hayes made extensive improvements in the conservatory, converting it to a promenade to distract dinner guests from whiskey and liqueurs.

as well as shrubs forming a background for seasonal changes of bloom.

Other than that, things seem pretty stable after all the comings and goings, plantings and uprootings of earlier administrations. Throughout our history, presidents faced with waging war or balancing the national budget have found that it's far simpler to have an impact on the White House grounds than on the U.S. Congress. The lawns today are dotted with thirty-four commemorative trees planted by the presidents. Now that the John Quincy Adams elm, a victim of disease, has been taken down, two magnolias planted by Andrew Jackson near the South Portico have seniority.

The White House gardens are open to the public two weekends a year, in mid-October and mid-April. Admission is free. For information, call (202) 456-2200. ☀

In the early nineteenth century, the White House garden featured a fancy French-style parterre to the south and Jefferson's pavilion to the west.

▼

They Called Her "Aunt Bumps"

Gertrude Jekyll (1843 – 1932) was more than just a garden designer. She was — and is — a gardening legend.

Jekyll (pronounced JEE-kill) was the mother of the lush, opulent English garden. Noted for her harmonious color schemes and bold foliage effects, she also emphasized a controlled layout and free planting (creating a sort of natural anarchy), maintaining a large plant list, and matching a gardening style to a particular site. If all that sounds very modern, it goes to show what we learned from Jekyll.

To Jekyll, trained in her youth as an artist, the garden was a palette. She called her planting plans "garden pictures" and compared the variety of plant shapes to brush strokes. An admirer of British painter J.M.W. Turner, she set out her plants in enormous clumps, creating the effect of an impressionist painting when seen from a distance.

A great designer in her own right, Jekyll also was capable of highly productive collaborations. Working with architect Edwin (Ned) Lutyens, who was twenty-six years her junior, as well as many other architects, she created some 350 gardens — most of them, unfortunately, lost today. (It was Lutyens's children who called her "Aunt Bumps"; she took them for rides in her trim, four-wheeled pony cart.)

Eccentric and energetic until her 89th year, Jekyll refused to travel and almost never left home, even to look at the gardens she was designing. She didn't need to. Intensely practical, Jekyll was highly attuned to detail; it's said she could explain down to the last pebble how to build a stone wall. To create her legendary designs, she was able to work strictly from architectural drawings of houses, demonstrating an amazing ability to evaluate space and light and remember visual images. The results have been described as some of the most beautiful gardens ever made.

She was a remarkable woman by any measure.

No wonder they're still evoking her name.

GOING NATIVE

Perfection is out, and "natural" is in.

After decades — even centuries — of Anglophilia, Anglophobia has arrived in America. If you've suffered from an inferiority complex regarding English border gardens, relief is at hand.

American garden design is going native. Or is it neonative?

Following nature's lead and planting native species gives you a sure-fire route to a stable, low-maintenance garden design while adding beauty to the landscape and conserving our natural heritage. Choosing native plants is particularly rewarding if you garden in a dry region — or any other area where growing conditions are extreme and conventional plants struggle to succeed.

Herewith, our six best ideas for going native in the garden.

If you garden in a dry region, choosing native plants is particularly wise.

▼

1 Let nature hardscape your garden. Before you begin to play with garden design, take a long look at the hand nature has dealt you. Are the landforms soft or jagged? Bright or subtle? Is the topography flat or varied? Take notes, then take the hint. Your goal in building walls or walkways is to re-create natural elements on a smaller scale, using natural stone in natural patterns — unless there is no stone, for then it will look out of place.

2 Take note of native plant groupings. Whether you decide to plant only natives or not, local plant masses provide an important example of what will succeed and look wonderful. Grow what already grows, or a variant of it.

3 Match the soil and the plantings. If your soil is acidic and your chosen plants need alkaline soil, you're in for a struggle. Work with nature and select plants that will thrive in the soil you already have.

4 Buy propagated wild plants from a reputable nursery. Seeing the collection of plants from the wild as a sort of shoplifting, "ecologically correct" nurseries have sprung up in every region of the country, offering both wild plants and information on how to grow them. Instead of collecting ever-scarcer native flora from the wild, you may want to support these nurseries by purchasing the stock they've propagated.

5 Blur the garden's edges. Unlike conventional gardeners, who may end plantings with an edge or a nice, tidy line, going-native gardeners aim to link their gardens to the larger landscape. To blend a garden's edges with the landscape, gradually reduce the planting density toward the perimeter of the garden, perhaps floating a few islands of plants into the wilder landscape to lead the eye outward.

6 Don't fertilize when you plant. Most wildflower communities thrive in areas of low soil fertility. Giving wild plants a big meal of nitrogen when you set them out usually is of tremendous benefit to surrounding weeds. Take it slow and easy at first. Mulch, weed frequently, and wait until the plants are established before you decide to give them supplements. Root growth should come first, so don't be disturbed if plants seem to be making a slow start. ☀

TRIMMING HEDGES NATURE'S WAY

The close observer who fully realizes the beauties of nature never looks on a hedge trimmed so as to show a level top and perpendicular sides without a feeling of disgust; and his sympathy goes out to the man who handled the shears with so little conception of either the beauties or the demands of nature.

Who ever saw a tree grow naturally with a perfectly level top, and limbs reaching just as far from the trunk at the top as at the bottom? When man demands of nature a change so great and so unnatural, she rebels and refuses to submit.

— *The Old Farmer's Almanac, 1894*

GOOD FENCES MAKE GOOD SENSE

They can be both attractive and supportive. Sometimes they even keep out the deer.

When you garden, you are not alone. Woodchucks, raccoons, rabbits, squirrels, deer, crows, and even field mice will be watching your garden from the very first moment you slam the back door and pick up a shovel. Their aim is to share your garden with you. Although you may feel philosophical about this at the start, the day some critter trims your 6-inch pea shoots to the ground is the day you will start thinking seriously about fences.

Americans have a love-hate relationship with fences. Our national spirit pleads, "Don't fence me in!" and coast to coast we treasure the concept of endless greenery stretching from front yard to front yard, neighborhood to neighborhood, unfenced. Yet we know that fences make sense — to enclose gardens, to exclude animals, to establish boundaries. Besides, fences and Americans go back a long way; we inherited the tradition from our European forebears, who have long had a tendency to contain their gardens.

So we compromise. We build fences not just as exclusionary devices but also as backdrops and important stylistic statements. We use them as supports and trellises for tomatoes, cucumbers, melons, pole beans, squash, peas, and other climbers. And we build more and more fences — out of every material we can get our hands on.

Wood has always been the most popular fencing material in America, from the civilized white-painted picket fences of early New England to the rough-hewn post-and-rail affairs worming across great stretches of the Midwest. For his fruit garden at Monticello, Thomas Jefferson specified a fence 10 feet high and so tight "as not to let even a young hare in." Open or closed, horizontal plank or upright picket, whitewashed or weathered, wooden fences have long been essential for protection against wandering livestock.

Wood is far from the *only* popular fencing material. The Victorians fancied metalwork fences outside their more urban homes.

Latecomers in the race to claim farmland in Washington Territory had to settle virgin forest. At first it seemed their main crop was stumps, and their farms became known as stump farms. Coming up with fencewood was not a problem. ▶

You may have to throw the switch to deer-proof your garden.

▼

Ranchers strung miles of barbed wire. Both amateur and professional gardeners have long grown hedges of every twiggy plant and have clipped them into shapes geometric and fanciful. One extension of that concept is the living fence, sometimes called the Belgian fence. This looks like primitive wattle fencing of interwoven poles but is actually rooted, and can be extremely handsome. (The same is true of open fences covered with grapes or other vines.)

But can it keep out the garden pests?

Wood, metal, barbed wire, hedges, living fences — all can add beauty to a homestead and offer other benefits as well. But when it comes to reliable, no-nonsense pest control, there's no substitute for electric fencing.

The ultimate deer-proof fence is sturdy, at least 6 feet high, and electrified. Some gardeners manage to exclude the critters with two strands of electric wire, one 6 inches and one about 2 feet above the ground. Just remember that if you install electric fencing, you must never let down your guard — or your current. As evidence, we offer the story of one gardener whose plantings were carefully guarded by electric fencing — until one day the power went out and the deer came in. You'd think they might have been fooled by past shocks and hesitant to keep testing the waters. You'd be wrong. It took them, the hapless gardener reports, less than 6 hours to catch on. ☀

Legally Speaking

In some parts of early America, fences weren't just an attractive addition to the front yard; they were a legal requirement. Residents of the colonial capital of Williamsburg, Virginia, were given 6 months to erect picket fences once their houses were built.

This Ha-Ha Is No Laughing Matter

When is a fence not a fence? When it's a ha-ha.

In the green English countryside, the pastoral urge is strong, and people enjoy looking out over their fields and lawns at grazing sheep or cattle. Only trouble is, you don't want the odd sheep to amble through the open French doors and into your parlor.

The solution to this problem is the ha-ha. Relatively little known in America, a ha-ha is a sunken fence or ditch dug at the edge of a property, usually with a reinforcing wall to guard against erosion. Its purpose is to separate two pieces of land without interrupting the view as an ordinary fence would.

Etymologists believe that the term *ha-ha* comes from the French interjection "ha ha!" expressing surprise. That's possible; you do come upon these sunken fences quite suddenly. But we suspect that anyone unlucky enough to fall into one while daydreaming would probably use stronger language to describe the event.

CHICKENS IN THE OUTHOUSE? GO WITH THE FLOW!

The birds will provide heat, the theory goes, they'll be hard to forget, and the eggs will be handy . . .

CALL IT AGROSYNERGY.

CALL IT NATURAL LANDSCAPING.

CALL IT ECOLOGICAL PLANNING.

CALL IT PERMACULTURE.

We've been hearing about the energy-efficient system for designed, sustainable agriculture called permaculture for some years now — ever since Bill Mollison, who coined the word, came over from Australia to spread it. Mollison's ideas have generated a great deal of excitement and some controversy. But what exactly is permaculture?

Permaculture is deliberate design, a strategy of long-range ecological planning that calls for fundamental changes in the way we treat the world around us. It begins at a philosophical level with questions about what we would make of a piece of land and goes down to the most practical considerations about planting peas and sheltering chickens.

To a great extent, permaculture is a program of laissez faire.

The Big Four

Our calling as gardeners is complex, and yet in a sense, it is very simple. In the end, plants want only four things:

1. PLENTY OF SOIL MOISTURE
2. PLENTY OF AIR IN THE SOIL
3. PLENTY OF PLANT FOOD
4. PLENTY OF SUNLIGHT

All we have to do is figure out how to give them these four essentials. In general, this means providing irrigation and proper drainage, mulch, fertilizer, cultivation, and the right location.

Land, Mollison observes, may yield more in its natural state than when plowed and fenced. Nature knows best. Thus, if we look at a particular site's history, its patterns of ecology, and the flow of life there, we can learn much about that site's resources and potential.

In permaculture, everything functions together, and it all works with, rather than against, nature. Tree crops and other perennial plants yield food while modifying climate and counteracting pollution. Buildings and fences form trellises for the garden. The garden feeds people and animals and hosts transient wildlife. The chickens, allowed to run free, eat bugs and fertilize the garden. Roosting in a combination outhouse/chicken house, they help heat the building and get frequent attention.

Scientist Mollison hails as his guru Masanobu Fukuoka, author of *The One-Straw Revolution*. Fukuoka calls for systems that take care of themselves and help each other. He does not plow, but broadcasts seeds in the season when they would naturally fall or lets plants reseed themselves. Instead of tilling or killing weeds, he uses mulch and rotates crops. His method of growing "involves little more than broadcasting seed and spreading straw," Fukuoka explains, "but it has taken me over 30 years to reach this simplicity."

In this spirit, you might install a barnyard pond that reflects warm light on a slope planted with fruit trees. The pond will host ducks that weed the garden and feed the family, supplying down, eggs, and eventually meat. Feeding on fallen fruit, the ducks fertilize the garden and control the pest population. In the orchard, chives and nasturtiums at the foot of dwarf cherry trees lure away or repel borers and aphids; they also spice salads. A steep slope is held with Saint Johnswort, an herb that provides pollen for bees (which cross-pollinate crops and make honey). And at the foot of the slope, coreopsis yields birdseed and helps control insects.

Such is life at Permaculture Acres. Part of the plan is to place gardens and activities in zones organized in roughly concentric circles in the landscape, working outward from the center of greatest activity, which is usually the house. If that's zone 1, then zone 2 would be the area immediately surrounding the house, the place for the chicken shed, gardens, and greenhouses, which need daily attention. Zone 3 would be the place for trees and somewhat self-sufficient crops. Zone 4 would hold the woodlot or berry patches.

Sound a bit like the old-fashioned family farm? Read more about it in Mollison's books *Permaculture One* and *Permaculture Two*, or just get started. According to Mollison, the answer to "Where do I start?" is "At your doorstep." ☀

LAZY DAISIES

The common yellow daisy or coneflower, planted around the house in patches, makes a very bright and pretty addition, and is especially desirable where one has neither time nor strength to cultivate a variety of flowers. These will come up year after year and need very little care.

— THE OLD FARMER'S ALMANAC, 1893

LANDSCAPING HINTS

- - - - - - - - - - - - - -

Everyone who has a pond near the house
should set a few water lilies in it. They
require very little care and yet are a
constant source of enjoyment during
several months in the year.

— *THE OLD FARMER'S ALMANAC, 1893*

At the turn of the century,
visitors pose on giant water lilies
in St. Louis's Tower Grove Park.

Plants have always had plenty of competition for the world's limited supply of water. In 1905, this natty motorist required water not only for his own refreshment but also to power his Locomobile steam car.

▼

EIGHT TIPS FROM A WATER MISER
What to do before *the tap runs dry.*

I n many populated areas of the world, the demand for water is increasingly threatening to outstrip supply. More and more, we're urged to conserve what we have, to water infrequently or not at all. Here are eight ways you can water less and grow more.

1. Zone Your Garden

Adopt a commonsense garden design by grouping plants according to their water needs. Don't put thirsty plants with those that need little water. It's not thrifty, and plants with low water preferences are actually harmed by overwatering. To collect water when it rains, set shrubs and species with greater water needs in basinlike depressions.

2. Put Your Foot Down

Water your lawn only when it needs it. A quick test is to step on the grass. If it springs back into place when you move, it doesn't need watering.

3. Choose Copers

Nature has developed many interesting and beautiful drought-tolerant plants. For a great many types of plants, there are drought-resistant alternatives. To find the ones suited for your garden, look around at what grows wild near you. Then look into those hardy plants that thrive and bloom their heads off in the arid regions of the world, taking lessons from the true deserts and the hot, dry mediterranean climate zones (which include parts of Chile, Australia, South Africa, and California, as well as the Mediterranean area itself). This applies even if you live in an area that receives ample rainfall, for virtually all gardeners must cope with dry stretches and with gardens that occasionally must be left untended, sometimes for weeks at a time.

4. Plant When It Pours

If possible, do most of your planting during the rainy season. Roots will go deeper into the soil and become better established.

5. Choose Your Time

Water according to a schedule and during cooler hours, when evaporation is slower. (Early morning is better than evening because the heat that follows during the day helps prevent fungal growth.)

COLOR SCHEMES FOR THE FLOWER GARDEN

In the garden, blue flowers should be placed next to orange, violet next to yellow, while red and pink should be surrounded by green or by white. White may also be dispersed among groups of blue and orange and violet and yellow flowers. Plants whose flowers are to produce a contrast should be of the same size.

— *The Old Farmer's Almanac, 1906*

6. Water Like a Connecticut Banker

Efficiently and conservatively, that is.

If you're planning a garden, install a specific, efficient irrigation system such as drip irrigation. When you're replanning, consider retrofitting to supply just the right amount of water to each area of the garden. It's smart to take advantage of zoning (see #1) and set separate lines into high, moderate, and low water-use zones, supplying water to the bases of plants to encourage good root growth.

7. Buck Up the Soil

The better and less compact the soil, the greater its water-holding capacity will be. Be sure to amend the soil with compost or peat moss before planting any shallow-rooted annuals or perennials. Weed promptly, before invaders can steal water from the plants you want. Don't fertilize healthy plants; it will only stimulate growth — and demand. Do try using a water-holding gel near roots. Polymers or gels (such as DriWater) applied to the root systems of plants can reduce water waste. All you have to do is add them to the soil and give them a stir.

8 . Keep Cool & Take Cover

Mulch is miraculous. Pile it over plant roots (but not stems). Mulched planting beds conserve moisture as they cool soil and reduce evaporation. Anything can be mulch. Don't rake up fallen leaves or needles under big trees; don't remove grass clippings. Mulch prevents weeds and slows erosion. As it decomposes, it improves the soil — see the Water Miser's previous tip.

Watering Wisdom

A 2,000-year-old bright idea is finally catching on in this country. Recent research has found that a technique called pitcher or pot irrigation is even more efficient than drip irrigation. To implement the system, you simply dig a hole in the area to be irrigated, place a porous (not highly fired) clay pot in the hole, and fill the container with water, either by hand or with a pipe or hose network. Fill the hole around the container with dirt. Water will slowly seep from the container into the surrounding soil.

A pot placed in the center of a ring of vegetables such as beans or peas will provide steady irrigation. Use two or three pots to water a shrub, or a ring of pots at the drip line to water a tree. Pitcher irrigation has been used in China for more than 2,000 years and is also used in India, Pakistan, and Iran. It has been studied and endorsed by David Bainbridge of the Desert Restoration Group at San Diego State University.

How to Keep Water from Running Down a Hill

It's heartbreaking to see water coursing down a slope without sinking into the soil. Sometimes it happens because the ground has become too hard and dry to absorb water. Sometimes the rainfall is too heavy, and the ground can't absorb it. In any case, here are five ways to help a hill hold water:

1 **With mulch.** Mulch the roots of plants growing on a slope; mulch will catch and hold moisture and improve water penetration.

2 **With air.** If the hill is planted in grass, aerate it in the fall. Rent an aeration machine if the area is large, or use a tined hand aerator (it looks much like a pitchfork). After aerating, rake up the plugs of dirt and grass, then mulch the hill for winter.

3 **With water.** Irrigate the hill according to a regular schedule. Either supply brief bursts of water and then shut off the supply or set a low-flow sprinkler to run for a long time (thus causing less runoff). Let the soil dry, but not to hardpan, which promotes runoff.

4 **With soil.** Terrace the hill with a series of retaining walls — an ancient design technique that makes sense both for creating planting areas and for conserving fertile soil.

5 **With plants.** Most drought-resistant plants have deep roots that reach into the soil to find moisture and hold soil in place. Ground covers are particularly effective in holding soil.

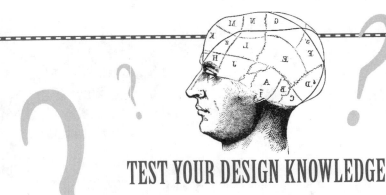

TEST YOUR DESIGN KNOWLEDGE

1 Match the letter of each term used in garden design with the number that corresponds to its correct definition below.

a. pergola _____
b. berm _____
c. espalier _____
d. gnomon _____
e. parterre _____

1. The part of a sundial that casts a shadow.
2. A fruit tree or ornamental shrub trained to grow along a flat surface, such as a wall.
3. An arbor or passageway with a roof of trelliswork on which climbing plants are trained to grow.
4. A garden in which beds and paths have been arranged to form a pattern.
5. A low, artificially formed mound of earth.

2 Frederick Law Olmsted (1822–1903) is considered the founder and most famous practitioner of American landscape design. He designed city parks, college campuses, and other famous open spaces, most of which we still enjoy today. Which of the following projects was *not* designed by Olmsted and his partners?

a. Central Park, New York, New York
b. World's Columbian Exposition, Chicago, Illinois
c. University of Texas campus, Austin, Texas
d. Biltmore Estate, Asheville, North Carolina
e. Connecticut State Capitol, Hartford, Connecticut
f. Mount Royal Park, Montreal, Quebec
g. Arnold Arboretum, Jamaica Plain, Massachusetts

CHAPTER FOUR

THE FLOWER GARDEN

"OFTEN I HEAR PEOPLE SAY, 'HOW DO YOU MAKE YOUR PLANTS FLOURISH LIKE THIS?' AS THEY ADMIRE THE LITTLE FLOWER PATCH I CULTIVATE IN SUMMER, OR THE WINDOW GARDENS THAT BLOOM FOR ME IN THE WINTER; 'I CAN NEVER MAKE MY PLANTS BLOSSOM LIKE THIS! WHAT IS YOUR SECRET?' AND I ANSWER WITH ONE WORD, 'LOVE.' FOR THAT INCLUDES ALL, — THE PATIENCE THAT ENDURES CONTINUAL TRIAL, THE CONSTANCY THAT MAKES PERSEVERANCE POSSIBLE, THE POWER OF FOREGOING EASE OF MIND AND BODY TO MINISTER TO THE NECESSITIES OF THE THING BELOVED, AND THE SUBTLE BOND OF SYMPATHY WHICH IS AS IMPORTANT, IF NOT MORE SO, THAN ALL THE REST. FOR THOUGH I CANNOT GO SO FAR AS A WITTY FRIEND OF MINE, WHO SAYS THAT WHEN HE GOES OUT TO SIT IN THE SHADE ON HIS PIAZZA, HIS WISTERIA VINE LEANS TOWARD HIM AND LAYS HER HEAD ON HIS SHOULDER, I AM FULLY AND INTENSELY AWARE THAT PLANTS ARE CONSCIOUS OF LOVE AND RESPOND TO IT AS THEY DO TO NOTHING ELSE. YOU MAY GIVE THEM ALL THEY NEED OF FOOD AND DRINK AND MAKE THE CONDITIONS OF THEIR EXISTENCE AS FAVORABLE AS POSSIBLE, AND THEY MAY GROW AND BLOOM, BUT THERE IS A CERTAIN INEFFABLE SOMETHING THAT WILL BE MISSING IF YOU DO NOT LOVE THEM, A DELICATE GLORY TOO SPIRITUAL TO BE CAUGHT AND PUT INTO WORDS."

— CELIA THAXTER, AN ISLAND GARDEN

Decoration Day,
May 30, 1899

TRAMPS & STOWAWAYS

Many of America's best-loved plants,
it turns out, aren't natives at all . . .

If America is a melting pot, so are her flower gardens — to an extent that few of us realize. Most of our cultivated plants (and nearly all of our weeds) are imports from other lands. The examples are sometimes bizarre, often fascinating: European cornflowers came to bloom in Pennsylvania after glass imported from Belgium was unpacked in a meadow there. In Connecticut, when a rubber reclamation factory stripped the waste from shoes and boots, it simultaneously deposited soil and seeds from the earth's four corners just before the fall rains; plants from all over the world took root. And German chamomile recently found a new home in Boulder, Colorado — where workers at the Celestial Seasonings tea-packing plant sometimes inadvertently carry home seeds in their cuffs and shoes.

Ever since the first Europeans landed on American shores, foreign plants have come along — intentionally or otherwise — for the ride. Some were lovingly imported, tucked into shawls or satchels; some were secreted in pockets and hems; others came virtually unnoticed, stowed away in packing straw or embedded in horses' hoofs. Some, unknown in this country a century or two ago, have changed the very look of the land. Consider . . .

Golden Bells

In the past 90 years, forsythia's neon-yellow sprays have become a ubiquitous sign of spring across much of North America. But that wasn't always the case. Before it became popular in America, before it had even been introduced in Europe, forsythia (also known as golden bells) grew wild on the South China coast. It wasn't until the mid-nineteenth century that, from the point of view of Westerners,

◀ Tramps and stowaways are often irresistible.

fortune found them. Robert Fortune, that is — a plant hunter for the Royal Horticultural Society of London, who disguised himself in native garb and pigtails to canvass the countryside for new plants. In 1846, the plant hunter carried a sample of forsythia to London, where it was named after William Forsyth, a founding member of the society and also the superintendent of the Royal Gardens at Kensington.

Forsythia made its way to America in about 1860, sailing from England to Massachusetts, but it did not appear in nursery catalogs until the end of the century. Since then, the hardy shrub has become known for withstanding northern climates like a crusty native, enduring pollution, high winds, and cold winters. Like its cousin the lilac, it does insist on resting in winter. Therefore, it does not do well in the Gulf states or the Southwest.

Dooryard Blues

Some people claim that the first American lilacs were imported directly from Persia to Portsmouth, New Hampshire, around 1695. The story goes that a cutting from one of these early bushes was later sent to George Washington at Mount Vernon. Whatever the source of the Mount Vernon lilacs, Washington went on record early with his observations of them: "Feb 10, 1786, Buds of lilac much swelled and seem ready to unfold." Even earlier, Thomas Jefferson had recorded in his garden book entry for April 2, 1767: "Planted lilac." They aren't native to this country, and they may not have come over on the *Mayflower*, but lilacs definitely were early immigrants.

And they kept moving. Lilacs (*Syringa*) reproduce rapidly with freely suckering stems. As settlers migrated west, so did the lilacs — thanks in no small measure to the countless itinerant venders known as plant peddlers. Packs on their backs, these professional Johnny Appleseeds followed the pioneers over the mountains and soon found that just as the homesteaders were ready to purchase pots and pans from other traveling salesmen, they also were eager to invest in shrubs and flowers that reminded them of home.

Today lilacs, both white and "old blue"— the name *lilac* is a corruption of the Persian word for indigo — have become a symbol of springtime in this country. Growing everywhere except the Deep South, they bring a fragrant dream of Oriental beauty to roadsides, parks, and gardens across America.

THE REFINING INFLUENCE OF CULTIVATING FLOWERS

Do not think it a waste of time to cultivate a few flowers, or to let the children have a flower bed. It is judicious for parents to cultivate a love of flowers in their children from earliest years, as flowers have a refining influence, and never lead astray, but always upward to what is purer and better. If one's time and strength are limited, a bed one yard square, with a geranium and a few nasturtiums, for instance, can give pleasure to the whole household; and these flowers will bloom all the season, until the frost blights them. A few flowers in pots are better than none.

— THE OLD FARMER'S ALMANAC, 1893

ALL THINGS CONSIDERED ...

A garden of hardy perennials is more satisfactory on the whole and less expensive than one of bedding plants, and they require less care than annuals. No one need refrain from having such a garden because the area of land is limited or because expense must be considered. The first cost of the plants is small, and practically, they last forever.

— *The Old Farmer's Almanac, 1916*

The Settlers' Companion

The tall, purple foxglove is a hardy plant, and it packs light for traveling: there are eighty thousand foxglove seeds to a single ounce. Each fall the wind shakes them out of their papery capsules and scatters them lavishly across the land. Rich in oil, starch, protein, and sugar, the seeds have a high rate of germination and thrive in well-drained, ordinary soil, sometimes forming large colonies in the wild (and creating a stunning sight on a remote roadside or in a forest clearing).

Foxglove (*Digitalis purpurea*, meaning "purple fingers") is native to Europe, where it has grown in gardens for centuries. When English and German settlers came to America, they brought foxglove seeds and scattered them on the edges of their homesteads. It didn't take long for the plant to escape the coastal settlements and begin the trek westward. In 1809, when John Bradbury set out to collect wildflowers in the newly acquired land of the Louisiana Purchase, he could trace the paths of the pioneers in the trails of foxglove they left behind.

More recently, the striking flowers became a clue for Russian prospectors, who noted that foxglove is an indicator of minerals in the soil where it grows. They began searching by helicopter for masses of the plant — and for the new iron deposits and coalfields the plants marked.

Long before it became the researcher's assistant, however, foxglove had been recognized as the physician's friend. As early as 1768, it was known to be a potent heart medicine. Raised today for the digitalin found in its leaves and seeds, foxglove is perhaps best known as the primary source of the commercial drug digitalis.

But you don't have to be a cardiac patient to appreciate the beauty of these purple masses of bells. Like other beautiful immigrants, foxglove adds one more dash of color and variety to its adopted land. As does another colorful traveler . . .

Roadside Ramblers

Orange-red daylilies came to Europe from China during the Middle Ages. They were brought to the New World in the seventeenth century and widely cultivated here. Today carefree, persistent patches of *Hemerocallis fulva* (the name means "beautiful for a day") blaze in deserted American cellar holes and form brilliant borders along country roads. In either spot, they offer living testimony to human history —for *Hemerocallis* spreads almost solely by division. Sometimes it's transplanted by gardeners. Sometimes it sends out underground rhizomes. Sometimes it appears unexpectedly, the offspring of the bits and pieces torn and tumbled along by snowplows or road graders.

In ancient times, the daylily was valued as both food — baked into a custard with rich milk, butter, and salt — and medicine — in the form of a poultice applied to burns. Daylily buds are edible, but today we use this proud plant most frequently to hold soil on hillsides and brighten those corners of the garden where a rugged, pest- and disease-resistant perennial is needed.

▲

Roadside ramblers really get around.

SEASONS OF A SUMMER FLOWER GARDEN

How to keep the color going all summer long.

A harmoniously arranged flower garden, often compared to an artist's palette, might much more accurately be likened to a symphony. A palette — or even a painting — is static, whereas the ideal summer flower garden develops in waves, reaches crescendos of bloom, and depends on chronological succession as surely as the British monarchy.

When planning your garden, choose flowers for their color, beauty, and fragrance, of course — but also consider the season in which they bloom. Avoid planting midsummer bloomers all in one spot; instead, distribute groups of them throughout the garden. This will draw the visitor's eyes through the whole area, creating the effect of a greater expanse of color.

Cupid plays makeup artist, putting the final touches on a pansy's face.

What combinations of plants will keep your garden
colorful all summer long?

Here are some suggestions.

Early Summer
(mid-May through mid-June)

Bleeding hearts
Delphinium
Early roses (*Rosa hugonis*; damask, eglantine, and gallica roses)
Iris magnifica
Oriental poppy
Peony

Midsummer
(late June through July)

Astilbes
Bee balm
Daylilies (try Stella de Oro)
Early-blooming white phlox
Hollyhock
Hollyhock mallow
Regal lily and Asian hybrids such as Enchantment
Snakeroot

Late Summer
(July through early September)

Asters
Fall-blooming anemones
Globe thistle
Harrington's pink aster
Japanese iris
Late lilies and daylilies
Monkshood
Pink and white phlox
Tiger lily
White *boltonia*

TULIPOMANIA

Seventeenth-century Holland had a bull market for bulbs.

One of the most bizarre incidents in floral history occurred in seventeenth-century Holland, when the Dutch tulip trade underwent a feverish period of speculation — one that makes the great stock market crash of 1929 look like a Sunday-school picnic.

Up until the sixteenth century, tulips were virtually unknown in Europe, although they were immensely popular in Turkey, where many species are native. (The word *tulip* is from the Turkish *dulband*, meaning "turban," because of the flower's resemblance to that type of headdress.) The first cargoload of bulbs to arrive at Antwerp in 1562 marked the beginning of the Dutch tulip trade that continues to this day.

The thing about tulips that fascinated the Dutch was the unusual habit called breaking exhibited by certain cultivated varieties (called breeders). In breaking — a phenomenon now known to have been caused by a virus transmitted by aphids — a monocolor tulip produces an entirely new variation that retains the color of the original flower only in streaks, or "flames." Once this break has occurred, the plant rarely reverts to its single-colored form, and the new variety can then be propagated for sale. A beautiful new color or pattern could mean big bucks for a lucky tulip trader.

Suddenly, almost everyone in Holland — from noblemen to peasant farmers — became a speculator in tulips. The Dutch called the phenomenon Tulpenwoede, or "tulip mania," and during the height of the craze (between 1634 and 1637), fortunes were both won and lost. A single bulb of one highly valued variety, the scarlet-and-white Semper Augustus, reportedly sold for 5,500 florins (close to $1,000 today, by some estimates). There was even one story of a cook who mistook some valuable tulips for onions and served his master, a bulb farmer, a stew worth 100,000 florins.

In 1637, Holland's tulipomania came to a crashing halt, although we suspect that even now there may be a few gardeners out there with a golden glint in their eyes, just waiting for their own "lucky break."

Note: For more fascinating stories about tulips and other ornamental plants, we recommend Peter Coats's book *Flowers in History* (New York: Viking, 1970), from which we learned about tulipomania. ☀

◀ No one had ever tiptoed through the tulips as Tiny Tim — ukelele in hand — did in 1968.

BLOSSOMS FOR BUTTERFLIES

Want to lure a few brilliant swallowtails to your garden? Here's how.

I t's obvious: butterflies and flowers were made for each other. As the poet pointed out, butterflies are flying flowers, and flowers are tethered butterflies. For those who want to entice a few flying flowers to their gardens, we offer some brief suggestions.

In attracting butterflies, it's important first to understand what they want out of life: nectar. The ancients, who believed that nectar fell into flowers directly from heaven, named it after the wine of the gods. Modern scientists explain, a bit less romantically, that nectar is the sweet, water-based fluid secreted by flowers to attract pollinators. It's neither a waste product nor a sap, but an edible treat made by a gland called the nectary.

Nature has made the nectary, the divine distillery, hard to tap. In some flowers, it's protected from rain by hidden hairs. In others, such as columbines, it's protected by the structure of the plant (spurs in the case of columbines). In most flowers, it's positioned so that pollinators must seek to sip or suck, deliberately probing with their tongues or some other mechanism. In the case of the butterfly, the mechanism is a tubelike proboscis — in *The Butterfly Garden*, author Jerry Sedenko compares it to a soda straw that can be coiled up when not in use.

Which brings us to the connection between butterflies and blossoms. Being sippers, butterflies fancy flowers that serve nectar in tubes. They also have extremely long legs and need a platform to land on. And they like to conserve energy. Many of the best butterfly flowers are not single blossoms but clusters of small blossoms arranged in a horizontal plane, such as daisies, yarrows, and Queen Anne's lace. Such an arrangement, Jerry Sedenko notes, allows a butterfly to load up on the nectar of many individual blossoms from one vantage point without having to flit from blossom to blossom.

But lots of the right flowers are only the first item on the butterflies' wish list. They also need fresh water, shelter from wind, and sunny open spaces — no wonder they find a wildflower garden irresistible, especially if there is a pond or brook nearby. Wildflowers provide butterfly baby food, too, and that's essential. If you don't offer food for the larvae, the grownups won't stick around long enough to lay their eggs.

For a nectar-rich flower border designed to satisfy these requirements, consider the plants listed below. Then invite a few butterflies over for a drink.

Nectar by the Spoonful

Asters
Bee balm
Butterfly bush
Butterfly weed
Clematis
Coreopsis
Cosmos
Foxglove
Fruit tree blossoms
Globe thistle
Goldenrod
Helianthuses
Honeysuckle
Hostas
Irises
Japanese anemone
Joe-pye weed

Lady's-mantle
Lavender
Liatris
Lilacs
Milkweed
Petunias
Phlox
Pussytoes
Queen Anne's lace
Rudbeckias
Salvias
Sedums
Sweet pepperbush
Thistles
Thymes
Verbenas
Yarrows

CALLING ALL VOLUNTEERS

Flowers that sow themselves are the answer to a busy gardener's prayers.

Pretty volunteers are almost always welcome.

▼

Self-sowing flowers are the busy gardener's reward for letting some plants go to seed in the fall. Even in colder areas of the country, many annuals and biennials reappear year after year — "volunteering," as the old-timers called it. Most gardeners soon come to appreciate those plucky, well-adjusted species. Volunteers provide an element of surprise, save money and effort, fill in bare spots, and often get a head start on annuals deliberately sown.

Characteristically, annuals produce a lot of seeds. After all, it's their biological imperative to move smartly through the life cycle and perpetuate themselves. You want them to do this — but not until you're ready. When a plant sets seed, as most gardeners know, it has less energy for blossoming. So continue deadheading until the second half of summer. Then, enough in advance of frost to be sure that the flowers will mature, allow seed heads to form on just a few plants.

Wind, birds, and gravity will do the rest, unless you choose to scatter the seeds in specific sites. It's interesting to see where they will pop up without your help, and sometimes this is the only way to get a plant started in an iffy spot such as a rock crevice.

In the spring, wait until seedlings have at least two real leaves before you pull them out or till them under. Seedlings you

GEE !! I WISH I WERE A MAN

I'd JOIN The NAVY

Howard Chandler Christy, hc

BE A MAN AND DO IT

UNITED STATES NAVY RECRUITING STATION

aren't expecting are often hard to identify, and nobody wants to discourage an enthusiastic volunteer.

Above all, enjoy your exuberant, impudent self-seeders. Don't worry about too much of a good thing — it's a lot easier to pull out what you don't want than to put in what you do. And if you'd like to encourage a little more volunteerism in your neighborhood, try some of these possibilities.

Annuals

Calendula and cosmos. Self-sown calendula always seems to be hardier than packet-seeded plants and certainly blooms more easily. Cosmos gets off to an earlier start when it's on its own than when the gardener plants it.

Floral Feeders for Hummingbirds

Even the most beautiful garden will be enhanced by the visit of an occasional hummingbird. These lovely creatures are particularly fond of bright — red, orange, or fuchsia — trumpet-shaped blooms. They like honeysuckle, red-hot poker, bee balm, and cypress vine (*Ipomoea quamoclit*), with its proliferation of red trumpets. Tiny hummingbirds consume more than half their weight in nectar (and insects) every day — so give them lots of flowers.

Love-in-a-mist. This old-fashioned favorite herb is sure to reappear. Save the seeds to sprinkle on breads.

Morning glories. In a mild year, these will winter over — as will alyssums, candytufts, cornflower, and larkspur.

Poppies. All sorts of poppies are prolific self-seeders. Try Iceland in cold regions; California, Flanders, and opium poppies in others.

Herbs

Borage. Once planted, borage is sure to come back, its fuzzy leaves easy to identify.

Coriander. It's so hard to keep coriander from going to seed that its self-seeding skills come as no surprise. The seedlings, however, are nondescript, so till carefully near last year's coriander until you can identify the volunteers.

Dill. Almost sure to self-sow, dill has the added advantage of being one of the easiest sprouts to recognize.

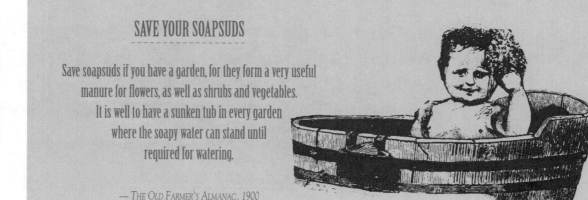

SAVE YOUR SOAPSUDS

Save soapsuds if you have a garden, for they form a very useful manure for flowers, as well as shrubs and vegetables. It is well to have a sunken tub in every garden where the soapy water can stand until required for watering.

— THE OLD FARMER'S ALMANAC, 1900

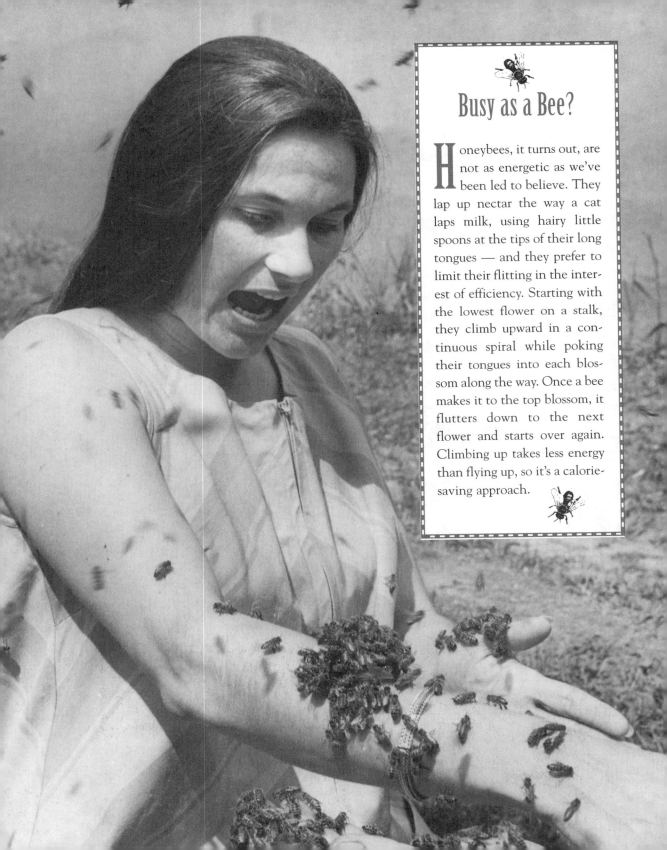

Busy as a Bee?

Honeybees, it turns out, are not as energetic as we've been led to believe. They lap up nectar the way a cat laps milk, using hairy little spoons at the tips of their long tongues — and they prefer to limit their flitting in the interest of efficiency. Starting with the lowest flower on a stalk, they climb upward in a continuous spiral while poking their tongues into each blossom along the way. Once a bee makes it to the top blossom, it flutters down to the next flower and starts over again. Climbing up takes less energy than flying up, so it's a calorie-saving approach.

THE CARNATION: SECRET AGENT OF FLOWERS

Today there are few cultivated flowers more common than the carnation (*Dianthus caryophyllus*), that ubiquitous fixture of floral arrangements that seems to fit almost any occasion (even St. Patrick's Day, when it's dyed a particularly unlikely shade of green). Earlier in its history, though, the carnation served a very different purpose, totally unrelated to its beauty or popular clovelike fragrance.

In the eighteenth century, the carnation became fashionable as a lover's flower, a symbol of hidden passion and secret confidences. Someone discovered that a message could be concealed in the carnation's calyx (the little leaflike structures at the base of the flower), to be read by the object of one's affection and hidden from the prying eyes of jealous husbands or disapproving parents.

The most famous story of the carnation's cloak-and-dagger past concerns Marie Antoinette, who remained imprisoned in the Temple, awaiting trial and execution, after the beheading of her husband, Louis XVI, in 1793. A bold young royalist, the Chevalier de Rougeville, somehow gained access to the queen's cell and "accidentally" dropped a single carnation at her feet. Marie read the message hidden under the flower, which outlined the knight's bold plan to rescue her, and used a pin to prick out a sign on the paper indicating that she had read and understood the note. Unfortunately for Marie, her jailers also discovered the paper and foiled the attempted jailbreak. Today the note is preserved in the French National Archives in Paris — bearing silent testimony to the carnation that almost saved a crown. ☀

◀ Who knows what secrets their carnations may hold?

Nocturnal seducer Morticia Addams could be membership chairman of the Night Garden Club. Meetings run late. ▶

FLOWERS THAT WORK THE NIGHT SHIFT

For a delightfully different garden, evening bloomers make great scents.

Most plants live for the daylight hours, when they can turn sunlight into energy and attract bees and other pollinating insects with their showy floral displays. But some plants operate on a very different schedule, waiting until night to open up their blossoms. There, in the dark, these flowers of the night send forth their sweet, heady fragrances — attracting not only humans but also nocturnal garden pollinators such as moths and beetles.

Instead of making your garden just a dawn-to-dusk attraction, consider planting a night garden especially of those flowers that love the dark. Look first for white or pale blossoms, and for the strong fragrance characteristic of night-blooming plants. This brings to mind images of jasmines and gardenias, but these subtropical shrubs are either too tender or too fussy for outdoor growing in most of the United States. Try some of the following plants instead.

- ☞ **Flowering tobacco** (*Nicotiana alata*) has long, tubular flowers that are creamy white and green on the outside and pure white on the inside. When they open in the late afternoon or evening, they release a sweet, jasminelike scent that attracts hummingbirds.

- ☞ **Moonflower** (*Ipomoea alba*) is a close relative of the popular morning glory and climbs with much the same vigor up a pole or trellis. Its large, pure white flowers are clove-scented and begin to open in the late afternoon. In warmer growing regions, moonflower is a tender perennial that can grow up to 40 feet in a single season.

- ☞ **Marvel-of-Peru** (*Mirabilis Jalapa*) has another common name, four-o'clock, which roughly corresponds to the hour it opens its blossoms. The plants grow 3 feet tall and sport dark green foliage and long, tubular flowers in white, red, pink, or yellow, often striped or mottled. A tender annual, Marvel-of-Peru blooms from midsummer until frost.

- ☞ *Gladiolus tristis* is a night-blooming variety with fragrant flowers that are yellowish white and marked with purple. Cultivars have red, yellow, or white flowers.

- ☞ **Evening primrose** (*Oenothera biennis*) is a hardy biennial that grows up to 6 feet tall and releases its sweet fragrance when its yellow flowers open in the late afternoon. The flowers form in succession and bloom over a long period of time. Evening primrose readily self-sows and can become invasive in a bed or border. To prevent this from happening, remove all ripening seedpods from the plant.

- ☞ **Evening stock** (*Matthiola bicornis*) grows about 15 inches tall and bears small lavender flowers that remain inconspicuous during the day but open toward evening or after a rain shower, releasing their powerful scent. This hardy annual blooms from midsummer into early fall.

- ☞ **Everblooming honeysuckle** (*Lonicera Heckrottii*) is an old-fashioned vinelike shrub that boasts beautiful purple trumpet flowers tinged a soft yellow inside their throats. Its blossoms last from June until frost, hence its common name. Like other night-loving plants, it releases its scent only at the end of the day, to perfume the evening air. ☀

GROWTH POWDER

A little finely ground bone mixed with the soil in a flowerpot is a benefit to the growth of the plant.

— *The Old Farmer's Almanac, 1893*

Planting by the Birds, for the Birds

A New Jersey gardener has developed an ingenious method for sowing the plants that resident birds find tastiest. She strings a line over a freshly tilled bed of soil. Birds perch and plant, via their droppings, seeds of the plants that they most enjoy.

As Hitchcock proved in 1963, it's even possible to attract a few more birds than you wanted . . .

A Simple Way to Make Candied Flowers

Candied flowers are terrific as simple but elegant decorations for cakes or desserts and are easy to make from the blossoms or petals of almost any edible flower. Certain rose petals, violets, mint leaves, and borage flowers are a few of the more popular candidates for candying, but experiment with other flowers, too, such as calendula petals or clary sage blossoms.

First, pick the flowers from the garden on a sunny day when they are fully open and dry. Remove the stems and lay the flowers or petals out on a double thickness of wax paper.

Beat one or more egg whites with a little water and carefully brush first one side of the petals or flowers, then the other, with the mixture, taking care not to coat them too thickly. Place the coated flowers on a sheet of dry parchment paper and sprinkle them on both sides with fine granulated sugar. Let the flowers sit for a day or so until they feel dry to the touch, turning them periodically and changing the paper if necessary.

Store the candied flowers in a single layer in a box lined with wax paper. Use them within 2 weeks. To decorate a cake, lightly press the flowers, petals, or leaves into the frosting in an attractive pattern.

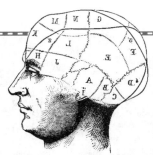

TEST YOUR FLOWER POWER

1 Which of the following flowering plants is not native to North America?

a. lupine
b. hollyhock
c. butterfly weed
d. eastern columbine
e. black-eyed Susan

2 According to folk wisdom, which of the following precautions should a person take to ensure a longer, happier life?

a. Never keep cut flowers in a bedroom overnight.
b. Never give a person a peony.
c. Never carry a bouquet of wildflowers indoors before May Day.
d. All of the above.

3 "What's in a name?" mused Shakespeare's Juliet. "That which we call a rose by any other name would smell as sweet." In fact, some flowers have several charming common names, some of which are little used today. Match the unusual flower names in the left-hand column below with their more widely used names at right.

a. Indian cress
b. heartsease
c. scorpion grass
d. plantain lily
e. deadmen's bells
f. ragged sailor
g. ephemera
h. wolfsbane

1. hosta
2. nasturtium
3. bachelor's button
4. monkshood
5. pansy
6. forget-me-not
7. lily of the valley
8. foxglove

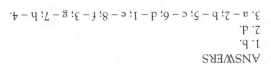

CHAPTER FIVE

GROWING FRUIT

"IT MAY BE SAID AT THE OUTSET THAT THE FRUIT ORCHARD WILL NOT 'LIVE BY FAITH ALONE.' IT REQUIRES WATCHFUL, INTELLIGENT CARE AND CONSIDERABLE INDUSTRY TO MAINTAIN THE FARM ORCHARD IN FIRST-CLASS CONDITION. WHILE THIS IS TRUE, THERE ARE FEW THINGS THAT BRING BETTER RETURNS OR GIVE GREATER SATISFACTION FOR THE LABOR BESTOWED. THE FARM WITHOUT ITS FRUIT ORCHARD IS LIKE PANCAKES WITHOUT MAPLE SYRUP — POSSIBLE BUT NOT ENJOYABLE. THE FARM ORCHARD SHOULD SUPPLY THE FAMILY AND FRIENDS WITH THE CHEAPEST AND MOST ENJOYABLE FRUIT THE YEAR THROUGH, AS WELL AS MANY DAINTY DISHES THE HOUSEWIFE KNOWS SO WELL HOW TO PREPARE."

— JOHN MCLENNAN, MANUAL OF PRACTICAL FARMING

Dorothy might say this apple tree has been a bit overstimulated.

HOW TO SAVE AN OLD APPLE TREE
Let's face it: you could hardly make it worse.

Few trees have more character than ancient, gnarled apples. But what if your backyard apple tree looks like it was planted by Johnny Appleseed — and ignored ever since? Not to worry. No matter how neglected and out of control a mature tree may be, it can probably be saved.

Where to start? There's no question: the path to salvation begins with careful pruning. When? Late winter or early spring is generally best, but a busy farmer once told us that "a good time to prune is whenever you can get around to it."

When you do get around to it, don't try to make up for years of neglect in one afternoon. Pruning stimulates growth, which is the reason experts often say that they prune as little as possible so that they'll have less to do later. Many experts advise a 3-year plan for saving a badly overgrown old tree: plan to remove one-third of the unwanted growth each year for 3 years. (Not following the "rule of three" involves three risks: sunscald from the massive dose of sudden, direct light; so much vigorous new growth that you have nearly as much to cut off again next spring; and a smaller crop of fruit, because apples bear fruit only on old wood.)

(continued on page 108)

FAMOUS YANKEE APPLES

The Baldwin, which must be regarded as, on the whole, the best of our New England apples, originated in the town of Wilmington, Massachusetts, and was named after Loammi Baldwin, the engineer who laid out the old Middlesex Canal from Lowell to Boston.

The Hubbardston Nonesuch originated in the town of that name in Worcester County. The Minister originated on the farm of a Mr. Saunders, in Rowley, Mass. The Porter was first raised by the Reverend S. Porter of Sherburne, Mass. The Williams originated on the farm of Major Benjamin Williams of Roxbury, Mass.

All these favorites were accidental. They have been, perhaps, somewhat improved by cultivation, but they were not the product of any attempt to create new varieties.

—THE OLD FARMER'S ALMANAC, 1888

WHERE & WHY TO PRUNE THAT TREE

A. Decapitate.
No apple tree needs to be more than 18 feet tall — 10 feet is better. Like the gods, you can punish those whom pride has raised up too high. Bring 'em down to where you can reach their fruit.

B. Let the Sun Shine In.
Branches that aim for heaven do nothing but shade those neighbors who, more generously, swoop toward earth with their bounty. Lop the high risers.

C. Pare Away All Crossed Branches.
Too many children in the playpen,
Too many piggies in the poke.
Apple branch crossing another,
My chainsaw does provoke.

D. Take Off Some Underbranches.
Down-growing branches are the ones you want to encourage, but not all of them at once. Be selective, show your good taste, pick, and pare.

E. Bind Up the Wounds.
Rotten cavities and cuts are open sores. Unless you feel a sympathy for bacterial life, gouge out the rotted wood and fill the cavity with pitch. No bandage necessary.

F. Water Sprout? Cut It Out.
Cutting away water sprouts is the family planning of apple tree rehabilitation. The poor old tree is trying to make babies, far more babies than it can raise up. Curb that urge.

G. Hey Sucka! Get Outta Town.
Root suckers should not be tolerated. They are new trees in the making, springing up from the roots of the old tree.

H. Massage the Media.
The topsoil under the tree, all the way out to the drip line, should be rototilled to remove competing sod.

I. Now Mulch.
Dress the entire rototilled area with compost to feed the roots. Hold back the compost a foot from the trunk of the tree to discourage rodents from camping out there and chewing on the tree.

J. Rest.
(Stop looking; there is no J there.) Take the rest of the day off. You have done good service, saved a tree, rebuilt an apple machine, and adorned your yard with a living structure that will be there after you're gone. Arboreal immortality.

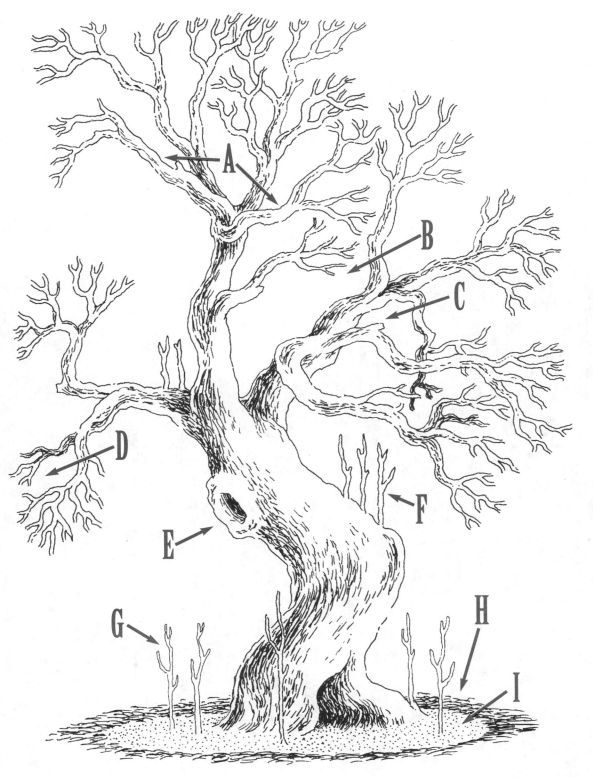

A good harvest yields apples for pies, apples for fritters, apple cores to feed the critters. Berkeley County, West Virginia, 1910.

So take it in stages, but do take it on. "The biggest mistake people make in pruning," says Catskill Mountain fruit expert Lee Reich, "is not to do it."

Begin with the parts that are clearly lost causes. If your apple tree has large areas of deadwood (easily spotted in late winter, when the buds on the healthy wood are swelling), cut it out. Deadwood is a doorway for disease. A rotted-out low branch, almost a second trunk, is common on old trees, and removing it is a job for a chain saw or a two-man crosscut. Remove it, or any large branch, in stages; make the final cut when you can use a free hand to prevent the bark from tearing as the branch comes off.

Next, look for any bad crotches — places where the tree forks into two branches of equal length and size. It's best to remove one of these,

or at least cut it back so that it becomes subordinate and heads off laterally. Cut just above the wrinkle where branch and trunk meet, not flush with the trunk, to leave a slight "collar" and the smallest wound possible.

Now aim your saw higher. When upper branches are allowed to grow vigorously, they often shade the lower ones. In addition, apple trees grow fast, up to 30 feet tall — well out of the average picker's reach. The best height for a backyard apple tree is about 10 feet. The shape is important, too. Most orchardists aim to give each tree a modified central leader (the predominant upper branch, the one that seems to be leading growth). To encourage this formation, cut back the top of the tree, leaving a somewhat horizontal branch as the leader. This lowers the tree, making it shorter and letting light — and pickers — in to the lower branches.

Speaking of those branches, it's time to prune them out, opening up the center of the tree to light. "Prune so the birds can fly through the tree in any direction," an old farmer advised us. This usually calls for a hand hook or, for very high branches, a pole pruner with a long handle. Cut out "suckers," the little branches that spring from the trunk or major branches. And cut out any snarls or tangles (sometimes called "mare's nests"). Your goal is to encourage the tree to grow out and down.

Branches that cross and rub, branches that grow too close together, and vigorous vertical branches that grow up from the main horizontal boughs — all should go. Keep in mind the "rule of three" and avoid large cuts, which will stimulate a rush of twiggy growth. Cut off inside branches before the outside ones.

As you proceed with your work, it's important to remember that a pruner is much like a sculptor and needs to take stock of the emerging shape of his or her project. Step back from your cutting frequently to see how the tree looks from a distance, and modify your approach accordingly.

Once you're comfortable with the overall appearance, you can move on to the details. Thin any crowded spurs — those stubby areas that bear most of the fruit and grow less than an inch per year. This will allow fruit to be evenly distributed along the branches. Invigorate a few individual spurs by cutting them back to strong buds. And cut away any root suckers at the base of the tree.

At this point, you're almost through pruning — almost, but not quite. Take a few extra minutes to scrape off any loose pieces of bark, and you'll not only improve the tree's appearance but also deprive insects of hiding places. This is a practice recommended by Lee Reich. "A good way to do it," he told us, "is to ball up chicken wire and run it lightly and carefully over the bark. [The bark] looks wonderful." ☀

LET US RAISE PEACHES!

The great mistake many peach-growers have made is in setting the trees too near together. They do well enough at first, but after a few years' growth the roots meet in the ground and rob each other of proper nourishment and plant food. A peach tree is a gross feeder. It makes wood rapidly and it requires abundant space, though a medium or even a poor soil is to be preferred rather than one too rich. With a rather poor soil, we can feed to it just what it needs, without the risk of overfeeding and a consequent tender growth of wood that is quite liable to winterkill.

—THE OLD FARMER'S ALMANAC, 1886

BACKYARD BANANAS
What's a tropical-looking plant like this doing in North America?

. . . SICH POP-PAWS! — LUMPS O' RAW

GOLD AND GREEN, — JES' OOZY TH'OUGH

WITH RIPE YALLER — LIKE YOU'VE SAW

CUSTARD-PIE WITH NO CRUST TO.

— JAMES WHITCOMB RILEY, "UP AND DOWN OLD BRANDYWINE"

Pawpaws, sometimes called "Hoosier bananas," rate high on our list of exotic natives well worth cultivating. Everything about pawpaws is improbable: their luxuriant, drooping, spear-shaped leaves; their funny, yellow-green tropical fruits (What are these doing in the Midwest?); even their taste and texture, so unlike most other Temperate Zone delicacies.

In fact, hardy pawpaws must have long ago strayed northward from the tropics and found a home in the rich river bottoms and uplands of the Ohio and Mississippi river valleys. They grow wild from New York State to northern Florida, and as far west as Nebraska, usually in thickets, for they have a habit of throwing up suckers from their roots.

Pawpaw trees, which are 30 feet tall at most, are long-lived; some have been known to survive 100 years and bear fruit for 60. Their odd fruits do look something like stubby bananas — but even more like smooth, green potatoes or enormous green peanuts. In flavor, pawpaws are also compared to bananas, but the likeness stops short. Ripe pawpaws are full-bodied, with flavors hinting surprisingly of vanilla custard, pineapple, and mango. There's nothing quite like them. They look and taste tropical, but they're hardy to minus 25 degrees.

With this kind of endurance, it's little wonder that no one a hundred years ago ever thought pawpaws would be considered exotic. At the turn of the century, the fruits were widely sold in markets and were so abundant in the wild that when much of the country's fertile bottomlands were commercialized, few folks bothered to save them.

If you're ready to reverse the trend, be sure to plant two for cross-pollination. Plant seeds or cuttings (handling the brittle taproot with care) in well-drained soil and partial shade. Pawpaws are easy to grow, and they shrug off diseases and pests. Recommended cultivars include Overleese, Sunflower, Fairchild, Taylor, and Ketter. ☀

Hardy pawpaws look like something straight from the tropics, but in fact they grow wild as far north as New York state.

▼

Elizabeth Testa, Miss Chiquita 1994. Unlike the tropical fruits in her colorful headdress, exotic-looking pawpaws can be grown even in the American Midwest.

Chiquita®
BRAND
BANANAS
1972
CELEBRATING 50 YEARS OF MISS CHIQUITA

THE ROMANS CALLED IT THE LOVE APPLE

This old-fashioned fruit has been everything from a symbol of fertility to a hair-setting gel.

Quince. Ancient Romans called it the "love apple," considered it sacred, and served it at wedding feasts as a symbol of love, marriage, and fertility. The early Greeks, too, held it sacred and associated it with women and love — an association that persisted in later cultures. Country people once thought that mulberry and quince should be grown together as husband and wife to ensure fertility for the land where they stood. Others believed that quince was the irresistible forbidden fruit eaten in the Garden of Eden, but that never stopped them from gathering the bright fruit and stewing it into sharp and flavorful jams and jellies. Quince made the original marmalade, for the word itself comes from *marmelo*, Portuguese for "quince."

It was the Portuguese who brought the first quince to the Americas, but it was the Pilgrims who listed quince as essential equipment for setting up a civilization in the wild. A few generations later, the pioneers carried the bright fruit west, adding a piquant touch to the perfect apple pie, cooking them into lovely sauces and preserves, and, oddly, making a gel for hairdressers by soaking quince seeds in small amounts of water.

Don't give up Dippity-Do, but do plant quince for its distinctive and delicate flavor. The woolly, pear-shaped fruit, related to both apples and pears, grows on deciduous trees that have exquisite, fragrant blossoms in spring. The trees adapt to almost any soil, require full sun, and are somewhat drought tolerant. Best propagated from cuttings and by budding, they are slow growers, so start with a young plant, which can either be formed into a tree or allowed to sucker into a bush.

Quince is inedible raw — the reason, some claim, that the fruit lost favor when so many cooks gave up preserving. When quince is cooked, however, the strong, musky flavor of the raw fruit is transformed into a sweetish peach-pear taste. Unless bruised, quince can be stored for months. In the words of a tenth-century poet, "[The quince] has the perfume of a loved woman and the same hardness of heart."

THE REAL JOHNNY APPLESEED?

The first fruit raised in this country was upon Governor's Island in Boston Harbor, from which on the 10th of October, 1639, ten fair pippins were brought up to the town. The words of the old record are, "there being not one apple or pear tree, planted in any part of the country, but upon that island." The island seems to have belonged, at that time, to John Winthrop, the first governor of the colony of Massachusetts Bay.

— *The Old Farmer's Almanac, 1888*

► Blue as a July sky and just as enticing.

THE BEST OF THE BERRIES
A handful of secrets for growing your own.

As trendy as raspberry vinegar and as old-fashioned as blueberry pie, berries are America's favorite fruits. Why do we love them? For their sweet compactness, their jewel-bright colors, and the fun of picking them — "one for the pucker, one for the pail." Planting berries makes sense even in a small garden, for few fruits are as easy to grow or produce as abundantly. Besides, although wild berries are still abundant, the cultivated varieties are generally bigger and easier to pick — and there's nothing like having a handful of heaven right outside your door.

The Secret of Planting Blueberries

"As big as the end of your thumb, real sky-blue and heavy." That's the way Robert Frost described them in "Blueberries."

No other berry quite matches the all-American blueberry, prized for its foliage (especially in the fall) as well as its fruit. All our native species are tough, hardy, and easy to grow even in northern climates — as long as they have strictly acidic soil. If you live in an alkaline area, consider growing them in tubs (sunken oil drums punched with drainage holes and filled with acidified soil); give them ammonium sulfate if their leaves turn yellow.

EASTERN REGIONAL RES
600 E. Merma
Philadelphia, P.
ment of Agriculture, Acri
ment of DEHYDRATED BLUEBERRIES
[ent of DEHYDRATED muffin mixes]
KING prepared can to
e in prepared 3 minute
ents of 3 and r
[simmer and prepar
in strainer with prepar
recipe 11
DBBCEPS 11
8/31/78
28 grams

▲

This preservation technique is still experimental, but explosion-dried blueberries can be reconstituted with boiling water for baking. Scientists say their flavor is almost identical to that of fresh berries.

Plant blueberries in the spring and in full sun. It's best, experts advise, to start with 2-year-old potted plants — at least two varieties for cross-pollination. And there's a secret to growing blueberries. These plants lack root hairs — the profuse, wispy roots that help most plants absorb water and nutrients — depending instead on a fungus that lives among their roots and does the same job. The secret of successful planting is to take a few handfuls of topsoil and leaf mulch gathered from nearby healthy wild blueberries and sneak them into each planting hole to inoculate the new plant. Tamp the soil down firmly around the plant and water it well. Water is very important — after all, berries are 85 percent water. Regular watering — as well as mulching to hold moisture — results in larger berries and can double the production of a bush.

A Better Strawberry

Modern strawberries are bred for color, cold tolerance, rot resistance, and transport — not characteristics to savor in a shortcake. But strawberries are easy to grow and definitely delectable when sun-ripened and picked really ripe. Maybe you already grow strawberries (and hate to weed them), or pick them yourself at a local farm. We have a proposal that's one degree more divine.

Tiny, compact alpine strawberries bear all summer long, don't send out runners (except for the Cresta variety), and can be started from seed. They also have an old-fashioned wild-strawberry flavor — distinctive and exquisitely sweet-tart. From frost to frost, alpine strawberries sparkle with white blossoms, red or white berries, and green leaves. They're rarely bothered by pests or diseases, are very drought resistant, and need only about 4 hours of sun a day.

Even if alpine strawberries didn't bear fruit, they would appeal to garden planners. They can be planted in a bed by themselves, but they are also ideal to mix with flowers, making a beautiful addition to a perennial border. Since they don't send out runners, they make great — and edible — edging plants. Set out a few dozen plants about a foot apart, and they'll make a lovely mounded hedge along the garden path.

Alpines are easy to grow from seed. Start them indoors in late winter, then set them out when each plant has at least four leaves and the danger of frost is past. Be sure to give them a steady supply of moisture. Once you have a stand going, you can increase your holding by dividing 2- or 3-year-old plants or saving seeds from mature fruits. Unlike seeds of many fruits, alpine strawberry seeds yield plants that are fairly true to type.

MANCHESTER.

KENTUCKY.

CAPT. JACK.

MT. VERNON, OR KIRKWOOD.

SETH BOYDEN, No. 30.

LONGFELLOW.

Grazers, take note! These berries are the best for eating out of hand. With a higher pectin content then regular strawberries, they also work well in any standard strawberry recipe — if you can beat the birds to your crop. One gardener we know has found a way: he plants white alpines and reports that so far the birds haven't caught on.

The Luxury of Raspberries

Raspberries are the aristocrats of the berry patch and have long been associated with rarity and luxury. (During his unsuccessful 1840 reelection campaign, President Martin Van Buren was evocatively attacked for "wallowing lasciviously in raspberries.") Fragile and perishable, they can be costly in markets, but if you grow them yourself, you may be able to wallow a bit — at least for the month of July.

Raspberry plants are very hardy and like sun. If you start them off in good soil and keep them mulched, they'll ask for no watering, no cultivating, and no weeding. "Keep their heads hot and their feet cool," one gardener told us. And keep them pruned—or your lovely berries will end up hidden in an impenetrable tangle of thorns. Pick raspberries when they readily fall off the bush and into your hand; if you have to tug instead of tickle, wait another day. ☀

Don't Shrug at Shrub

Have you ever sipped raspberry shrub? This old-fashioned sweet-and-sour beverage was a favorite of farmers making hay in raspberry season, but you can make it with frozen berries and enjoy it all year round.

Combine 1 cup white vinegar, 1 cup water, and 1 quart raspberries with 3 cups sugar. Let the mixture stand until the sugar melts and the berries give up their juice. Then heat the mixture until it starts to boil. Remove it from the heat, strain, and allow to cool. Serve over ice, diluted with water, seltzer, juice, or ginger ale. Makes about 2 quarts.

Blackberries: The Opportunists of the Berry Patch

There were only a few species of blackberries in America when the country was first settled, but clearing the land for farming apparently created a situation of natural hybridization. Even today we notice that blackberries are among the first shrubs to take over recently burned or logged land; as children, we knew to follow the logging roads, berry pails in hand.

Cultivated, homegrown blackberries give higher yields than those in the wild and produce larger berries that many consider more flavorful. (Many also are thornless.) Since different cultivars have highly variable temperature preferences, be sure to choose one that's tried and true for your region. Give the plants good soil and sufficient moisture, and they'll bear enough for jams, jellies, pies, juice, and eating fresh.

OLD-FASHIONED BERRIES WORTH ANOTHER LOOK

Gooseberries are the stuff of fools, and mulberries the subject of nursery rhymes. But don't write them off . . . .

Few of today's children would know the plant if they fell into it — but "Here We Go 'Round the Mulberry Bush" is still heard in schoolyards and playgrounds across the nation.

Both gooseberries and mulberries are great, easy-to-grow berries suffering from bad press. Gooseberries sound silly and are sometimes sour; mulberries are messy — really messy when dead ripe — and they stain your clothes.

But oh! The flavor of a choice cultivar! There's a huge difference between a good-quality cultivar of gooseberry (such as Poorman, Silvia,

or Clark) and a sour one with a tough skin. Some wild mulberries can be cloyingly sweet, but many domesticated varieties (try Illinois Everbearing, for one) have a tart edge.

In medieval times, mulberries were used to dye fabrics — and their syrupy juice can stain the lips, hands, feet, and clothing of enthusiasts who consume them with casual gusto. They're very soft and perishable, delicious right off the bush, but they also can be used for wine, preserves, or tarts. Be warned: don't wear your finest when you dance around the mulberry bush.

Gooseberries, neater to consume, inspire similar enthusiasm. Gooseberry lovers have been known to drive major distances and commit minor crimes for a taste of the sweetish berry, especially cooked into gooseberry pies, cobblers, tarts, preserves, and fools. Gooseberries of one variety all ripen at once, so they may be picked in one day. When fully ripe, they are delicious eaten fresh.

Eighteenth-century England gave rise to a gooseberry-raising mania that concentrated mainly on size — and at its height, in the mid-nineteenth century, resulted in berries the size of small apples. In America, gooseberry breeding came to a halt in the 1920s, when the berries were implicated in the spread of the white pine blister rust fungus, and a federal law restricted their cultivation. Although wild varieties proliferate and gooseberries are not very susceptible to the disease (the federal ban was lifted in 1966), some states still restrict growing. So before planting them, consult your state agricultural agent to make sure they are allowed in your area.

If you decide to grow gooseberries, choose a site carefully — a plant can live for 20 years or more. These berries need good air circulation but tolerate shade and usually thrive in areas where summers are cool. Mulching is helpful, and some pruning is necessary, but in general gooseberries are not demanding. As new generations taste some of the sweet cultivars, we predict a resurgence in the popularity of these delicious old-fashioned fruits. ☀

THE CULTURE OF THE GRAPE

Every farmer, and every owner of a cottage with a rod of land, ought to cultivate a few choice grapes. They require but a small space; they are ornamental, either pruned as a shrub or trained as a vine; they are among the most healthy and luscious of all our fruits; and with proper care and attention, they produce an annual crop equal to any other in money value.

—*The Old Farmer's Almanac, 1861*

GRAPES FOR THE BACKYARD GARDENER

If you've never tasted homegrown grapes, you've never tasted grapes.

I n Greek mythology, King Tantalus was condemned to stand in water that receded when he tried to drink, and beneath bunches and bunches of grapes that the wind blew away when he reached for them. Poor Tantalus. Robbed of the sheer pleasure of eating homegrown grapes.

But it's a pleasure you can enjoy — and should. And don't stop with the standard Concord. If you've ever tasted Interlaken, Van Buren, Canadice, or Niagara, you already know there's more to life than supermarket grapes. Much more. Grow them for their dependability. Grow them for their productivity. But most of all, grow them for their taste. And keep these pointers in mind.

What Do Grapes Need to Flourish?

☛ Air and full sunlight, to begin with, which is why grapes climb. They like to be trellised and will thank you for it, but they also will climb young maples, old bedsteads, and stone walls. An Oregon gardener reports that her grapes grow best on fir trees. Wherever you grow them, make sure your grapes have good air circulation to prevent fungal disease and encourage pollination.

☛ Regular pruning. Be brave and hack away with goodwill in late winter; aim to keep fruit and cane in balance. For each vine, save about four canes (the year-old wood of the plant), because that's where the new fruit will grow. By each cane, leave a spur — a cane pruned down to a couple of buds — which will provide the next year's fruiting canes. It's far better to prune as best you can than never to prune at all.

☛ Judicious feeding. Begin each season with a good dose of nitrogen-rich fertilizer. Thereafter, if your vines are producing admirably, feed them sparingly, or they may run to brush, which winterkills easily. Grapes need potassium and are quite fond of nitrogen, but when you fertilize, do so widely. Their roots stretch horizontally up to 8 feet from the main stem, and they go deep in search of water, which is why grapes don't mind a dry year.

▶

Poor King Tantalus — tantalized forevermore.

What Will You Get?

☞ Beautiful vines to cover an arbor or fence, providing shade and privacy. Let the canes ramble a bit if you want more foliage. A canopy of grape leaves provides natural cooling for a patio — or train them over a roof for air conditioning.

☞ Plenty of excess vines to make into wreaths and baskets.

☞ Broad, mild-tasting leaves to stuff with rice or lamb and spices for delicious Middle Eastern dolmas. (Poach the leaves first if they're not so young and tender, and store plenty in brine for later use.)

☞ Fragrant blossoms that wind pollinate.

☞ Bunches of sweet, juicy fruit.

What Can You Do with the Fruit?

☞ Eat it out of hand (grapes keep well under refrigeration for many weeks if they are dry and the temperature is set just above freezing).

Grape Pie

If you grow seedless grapes, try putting them in a delicious pie. Here's what you'll need:

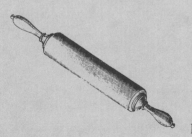

6 CUPS SEEDLESS GRAPES
6 TABLESPOONS HONEY
3 TABLESPOONS TAPIOCA
1 TABLESPOON BUTTER
1 TEASPOON LEMON JUICE
PINCH OF SALT
DOUBLE CRUST FOR A 9-INCH PIE

Preheat the oven to 375° F. Stir together the grapes, honey, tapioca, butter, lemon juice, and salt. Pour the mixture into the bottom pie crust, top with the other crust, and bake for about 40 to 45 minutes, or until golden brown. Cool for at least 10 minutes before serving. Serves 6 to 8.

☛ Dry the grapes, turning them into — of course — raisins.

☛ Freeze them for later use. (They will soften but will retain their flavor.)

☛ Squeeze the grapes for juice and jelly, or, if they're seedless, make grape pie (see box). To make jelly, first wash the grapes, discarding any floaters. Cook the washed grapes in a small amount of water until their skins burst. Drain them over a kettle in a jelly bag or a square of clean sheeting. "Don't squeeze," Mother told us; "it will make the juice cloudy"— but a careful squeeze will hasten things. Measure the juice and add ½ cup sugar for every 2 cups juice. Boil the mixture until it sheets from a spoon, and it will invariably jell. Well, almost invariably. Grapes are high in pectin, so if they're too ripe, it's best to forget about the jelly or add a package of Sure-Jell. You'll get about 5 pints of jelly for every 6 cups of juice. ☀

We Heard It Through the Grapevine

Although there's every good reason for growing grapes, the decision to do so is up to you. Not so in early Virginia, where in 1716 the Colonial Assembly passed a law requiring every householder to plant at least ten grapevines.

The Man Who Developed the Concord Grape

It wasn't easy.

From the time the first European settlers in North America tasted the native species they dismissed as "fox grapes" and "bullet grapes," the search was on for something better. For literally centuries, plant breeders and amateur viniculturists all over America experimented with alternatives. They developed a total of two thousand new kinds of grapes, but nearly all were inferior to European varieties.

All, that is, until Ephraim Wales Bull produced the first Concord grape — named for Concord, Massachusetts, where Bull lived most of his life —in 1849. Bull was not an overnight success — he painstakingly grew twenty-two thousand seedlings before coming up with the Concord — but he was undeniably a success. Or at least his grape was.

The Concord became the first grape to be grown in America on a commercial scale, and it's still the best-known variety in this country. "A grape for the millions," Horace Greeley called it. But Bull himself was widely recognized for his achievement only late in life and profited little from it even then. With no patent protection available for plant developers, he lost control of commercial development almost immediately. He died embittered and in poverty; "there are no honest nurserymen," he once lamented. Today, in Concord's Sleepy Hollow Cemetery, Ephraim Bull's grave bears a simple epitaph: "He sowed — others reaped."

Peaches! Preposterous piles of round, rosy peaches plump as pillows, sweet as summer, and with juice enough to run down your chin.

THOMAS JEFFERSON'S FAVORITE FRUITS

Above all others, the president preferred peaches.

HE HAD LAWNS, HE HAD BOWERS,
HE GREW FRUITS, HE GREW FLOWERS,
THE LARK WAS HIS MORNING ALARMER . . .
— "FARMER'S ARMS" (AUTHOR UNKNOWN)

Thomas Jefferson — idealist and revolutionary, architect and author, president and gardener — was seldom lukewarm about anything. When it came to growing fruits, he was passionate. Constantly experimenting, Jefferson grew 170 varieties of fruits at his beloved Monticello. He also kept detailed records about every aspect of his estate — right down to the number of garden peas he got to a pint (twenty-five hundred). Peter Hatch, Monticello's current director of grounds and gardens, and his staff are scarcely less thorough. Working from the president's writings and their own research, they've identified many of Jefferson's favorite fruits and brought them back to Monticello. Here's what they've found.

Above all fruits, Jefferson preferred peaches, and in his time he tried out 38 varieties of them. By 1811, Monticello's South Orchard contained 163 peach trees, and thousands more served as ornamental fences for his fields. The trees thrived at hot, humid Monticello. Jefferson and his many guests devoured peaches while they were fresh and ate them dried in the winter. Slaves distilled peaches into mobby, or peach brandy. They probably, like their neighbors, fed peaches to the hogs. They even used peaches as fuel for the fire.

Introduced into Florida as seeds by the Spanish conquistadors in the sixteenth century, peaches had been spread north by nature and Native Americans in such quantity that early botanists thought the Southeast was overrun with wild peaches. Yet few cultivars were available in Jefferson's time. Always on the lookout for variety, he planted such peaches as Heath Cling, Oldmixon Free, and Indian Blood, all of which are once again growing at Monticello today.

Unlike peaches, apples were available to Virginia gardeners in hundreds of varieties in Jefferson's day. The master of Monticello experimented with some seventeen varieties but concentrated on only four. He favored Esopus Spitzenburg and Newtown Pippin for eating and Hughes' Crab and Taliaferro — particularly Taliaferro — for cider. He called it "the best cyder apple existing," "nearer to the silky Champaigne than any other."

Jefferson kept meticulous records about everything — including the first and last appearances of 37 varieties of vegetables in the Washington market during the eight years of his presidency.

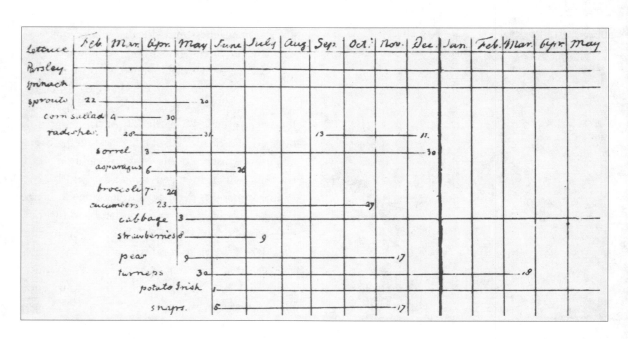

Unfortunately, the Taliaferro apple has disappeared from cultivation, but the orange-flecked Esopus Spitzenburg and pineapple-flavored Newtown Pippin (both New York Staters by origin) have survived. Writing from Paris, Jefferson declared that the French had "no apple to compare to our Newtown Pippin." Queen Victoria liked the Pippin so much that she lifted the import duty on all American apples, and the Pippin was exported to England in great quantity for many years.

Peaches and apples were only the beginning. Jefferson experimented with fruits of all kinds and was not one to spare the superlatives when he found a variety he liked. Among his other favorites:

☛ **Apricots:** The Peach (of course).

☛ **Cherries:** The Carnation. Jefferson grew eighteen varieties of cherries at Monticello but considered the Carnation "so superior to all others that no other deserves the name of cherry."

☛ **Figs:** The Marseilles, a white variety he called "incomparably superior to any fig I have ever seen" and still very productive at Monticello.

☛ **Pears:** The bite-size Seckel, which originated near Philadelphia. ("They exceeded anything I have tasted since I left France," he declared, "& equalled any pear I had seen there.")

☛ **Plums:** The greengage (although he tried twenty-six other varieties as well).

Jefferson was not a man to pick a fruit lightly. The fruit gardens at Monticello were his experimental laboratory, and he tended them for 50 years with characteristic curiosity and enthusiasm. If you'd like to follow in his horticultural footsteps, you can start by requesting a price list from the Thomas Jefferson Center for Historic Plants, Monticello, P.O. Box 316, Charlottesville, VA 22902. ☼

▲

"Planting is one of my great amusements," Jefferson admitted.

A PLANTSMAN FOR THE PEOPLE

Northern gardeners have a friend in Elwyn Meader.

When we called to talk to Elwyn M. Meader about the Reliance peach, he was out — way out in the blueberry field. Meader, who has been retired from the horticultural department at the University of New Hampshire for more than 25 years, is still doing what he does best: growing and breeding plants.

If you garden in the North, you're more than likely already raising one of Professor Meader's varieties: perhaps the Meader blueberry or the Sungold casaba melon, the Royalty purple bean or the ice-blue Miss Kim lilac. But the fruit for which Meader is best known is the Reliance peach.

Professor Meader first got acquainted with peaches during his student days in New Jersey. In about 1948, he experimented with a white-fleshed peach from Minnesota and a yellow-fleshed southern peach called the Oriole. Crossing those two, he selected the yellow-fruited offspring. By the time the second generation came along in the 1950s, Meader was working at the University of New Hampshire in Durham, near the town where his ancestors had farmed for a couple of hundred years and where he himself had grown up.

Winters are tough in New Hampshire, even in the coastal area, but Meader's peach trees were standing up to them. In late January of 1962, temperatures fell to 25 degrees below zero. The next summer, one of the seedling trees produced a peck of perfect peaches.

"I was amazed," Professor Meader says. "That one got named Reliance."

In the past 30 years, the Reliance peach has made its way around the world. Widely available in nurseries, it succeeds as far north as Maine and southern Quebec. A record freeze in Pennsylvania a few years ago destroyed the entire commercial peach crop — except for the Reliance peaches.

We've often thought that peaches are like tomatoes, in this respect: anyone who's eaten a vine-ripened, homegrown tomato knows its superiority to the supermarket sort. Anyone who's eaten a tree-ripened peach knows the same thing. Home-grown peaches? "There's nothing like them," Professor Meader says. "Some of those on the market — they've got no more taste than a cork stopper."

He ought to know; he's the man who made something better. And his fame has spread along with his peach. "About a week after the iron curtain went down," Meader reports, "I got a letter from Romania. 'Please send us the Reliance peach,' it said. It's made a lot of people happy." ✺

AFFORDABLE LUXURY

The cultivation of choice fruit has a tendency to promote the health and happiness of a family, affording a greater luxury, and a better, than the imported fruits.

—*The Old Farmer's Almanac*, 1846

◀

Fields, hillsides, cellars, and barns are Elwyn Meader's laboratories.

At a doll's tea party, rhubarb pie is much more palatable than pills.

Rₓ RHUBARB

Henry VIII took rhubarb root on his deathbed. (Apparently it didn't do him much good. . .)

The sour tang of rhubarb is, for many home gardeners, one of the real highlights of the growing season. Appearing earlier in the spring than most other crops, the red-and-green stalks have long been considered a "tonic" that helps to raise the spirits at a time of year when the palate is bored with winter vegetables and yearning for a taste both fresh and stimulating. Whether it is baked in pies or tarts (another common name for rhubarb is "pie plant") or stewed with sugar and lemon zest, rhubarb, though considered a minor crop by most people today, is for many traditional gardeners "just what the doctor ordered."

In fact, for thousands of years, the dried and powdered roots of medicinal rhubarbs (*Rheum officinale* and *R. palmatum*, both distant cousins of modern garden varieties) have been prescribed by physicians as a gentle and effective purgative and astringent that can either cleanse or "bind" the body depending on how it is used.

The Romans gave us the word *rhubarb*, which is derived from the Latin word *rhabarbarum* — *Rha* being an ancient name for the Volga River, and *barbarum* referring to the fact that rhubarb was native to foreign (Asian) lands that the Romans considered uncivilized.

After the Middle Ages, rhubarb became even more available in Europe, and a kind of "rhubarb fever" broke out, setting plant explorers to exploring,

traders to trading, and doctors to prescribing. King Henry VIII took rhubarb root on his deathbed in 1547. Rhubarb pills also were prescribed for a time as a cure for syphilis, as well as rickets, itching, leprosy, freckles, and "all continual Feavers of what kind soever." Even English dramatists commented on the popularity of the drug, with Shakespeare's besieged Macbeth asking, "What rhubarb, senna, or what purgative drug/Would scour these English hence?"

In the years 1768 and 1769, London imported some 60 tons of the roots. In fact, the British, keen gardeners that they are, led in the quest to establish the "true" medicinal rhubarb from seed. Since rhubarb does not always breed true from seed, and since different varieties can cross-pollinate and hybridize quite readily, this was no easy task. Also, the English climate seemed to foil the best efforts of plant breeders, until at last one species, *Rheum palmatum,* was declared the "true rhubarb" in 1769, and cultivation of it spread like wildfire from London to Moscow.

By the early nineteenth century, though, British gardeners found themselves faced with another dilemma: what to do with all the rhubarb that wasn't the "true" medicinal stuff? In the spring of 1808 or 1809, a nurseryman named Joseph Myatt decided to bring five bundles of rhubarb to market in London. He sold only three. It took a while for the sour (some people called it "mediciney") taste of rhubarb to catch on, but once it did, England experienced another Rhubarb Revolution, this time using the fruit as food rather than medicine. By the 1840s, Myatt's son William had planted 20 acres in rhubarb and was sending three wagonloads at a time to market. The same cross-pollinating tendencies that had made rhubarb so hard to grow true from seed now aided plant breeders in developing bigger, tastier, and earlier hybrid cultivars with names such as Scarlet Goliath and Crimson Perfection. Garden rhubarb as we know it had arrived.

Today Washington State grows the largest percentage of the small commercial U.S. rhubarb crop, most of it destined for freezing, canning, and processing plants. But home gardeners know that nothing can compare to the fresh item. Rhubarb requires little attention, just a top dressing of manure once a year, and in return it provides years' worth of pies, preserves, and "spring tonics" guaranteed (in a long and great medical tradition) to be a sure cure for whatever ails you.

Note: True rhubarb aficionados will want to consult Clifford M. Foust's definitive book on the subject, *Rhubarb: The Wondrous Drug* (Princeton, New Jersey: Princeton University Press, 1992) for more information. ☀

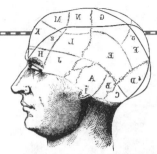

TEST YOUR FRUITFUL KNOWLEDGE

1 For each of the following definitions, supply the appropriate word or phrase that contains the name of a common fruit.

a. legislation that protects used-car buyers (two words)
b. spring training association of baseball teams (two words)
c. old-style theatrical illumination, or the focus of attention
d. derogatory term for a Latin American dictatorship (two words)
e. a rude, derisive facial gesture, also known as a "Bronx cheer"

2 The tangelo appears in markets every year. It is a hybrid, and it doesn't take a rocket scientist to surmise that one of its parents is the tangerine, or mandarin orange. But which of the following citrus fruits is its other parent?

a. orange
b. lemon
c. grapefruit
d. citron

3 Fruits figure largely in myths, traditions, and fables. Name the persons involved in the following famous stories.

a. He supposedly discovered the law of gravity when he was conked on the head by an apple.
b. Old Testament king whose wife, Jezebel, ordered the murder of Naboth for his refusal to give up his vineyard to the king.
c. He chopped down a cherry tree and couldn't lie to his father.
d. Huntress of Greek myth who lost a footrace when she stopped to pick up three golden apples.

ANSWERS

1. a – lemon law; b – Grapefruit League; c – limelight; d – banana republic; e – raspberry.
2. c. Another name for the grapefruit is pomelo, and tangelo is a compound word formed from tangerine and pomelo.
3. a – Isaac Newton; b – Ahab; c – George Washington; d – Atalanta.

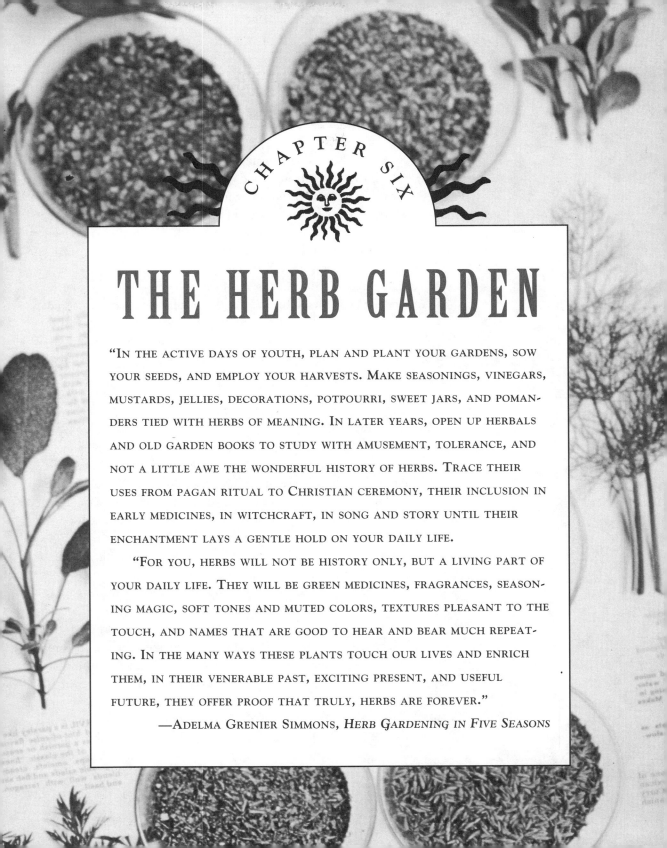

CHAPTER SIX

THE HERB GARDEN

"IN THE ACTIVE DAYS OF YOUTH, PLAN AND PLANT YOUR GARDENS, SOW YOUR SEEDS, AND EMPLOY YOUR HARVESTS. MAKE SEASONINGS, VINEGARS, MUSTARDS, JELLIES, DECORATIONS, POTPOURRI, SWEET JARS, AND POMANDERS TIED WITH HERBS OF MEANING. IN LATER YEARS, OPEN UP HERBALS AND OLD GARDEN BOOKS TO STUDY WITH AMUSEMENT, TOLERANCE, AND NOT A LITTLE AWE THE WONDERFUL HISTORY OF HERBS. TRACE THEIR USES FROM PAGAN RITUAL TO CHRISTIAN CEREMONY, THEIR INCLUSION IN EARLY MEDICINES, IN WITCHCRAFT, IN SONG AND STORY UNTIL THEIR ENCHANTMENT LAYS A GENTLE HOLD ON YOUR DAILY LIFE.

"FOR YOU, HERBS WILL NOT BE HISTORY ONLY, BUT A LIVING PART OF YOUR DAILY LIFE. THEY WILL BE GREEN MEDICINES, FRAGRANCES, SEASONING MAGIC, SOFT TONES AND MUTED COLORS, TEXTURES PLEASANT TO THE TOUCH, AND NAMES THAT ARE GOOD TO HEAR AND BEAR MUCH REPEATING. IN THE MANY WAYS THESE PLANTS TOUCH OUR LIVES AND ENRICH THEM, IN THEIR VENERABLE PAST, EXCITING PRESENT, AND USEFUL FUTURE, THEY OFFER PROOF THAT TRULY, HERBS ARE FOREVER."

—ADELMA GRENIER SIMMONS, *HERB GARDENING IN FIVE SEASONS*

THE GARDENER'S PHARMACY

Some people look to the drugstore to relieve their suffering. Others head out to the herb garden.

Interest in the medicinal value of herbs is keen these days, not only among the descendants of midwives and folk healers but also among medical researchers and government officials worldwide. That, of course, doesn't mean you should empty the medicine cabinet when you plant an herb garden. In some cases, modern medicines are superior to herbal remedies, and in other instances herbal cures have proved ineffective or even dangerous. They are not a substitute for a visit to the family doctor. Still, there is considerable overlap between the farm and the pharmacy. About 25 percent of all prescription drugs sold in the United States today contain at least one major ingredient that can be raised in the garden. If you'd like to try some homegrown remedies for minor aches and pains, consider these common backyard herbs.

Glorious Garlic

Traditionally a hot-climate crop, garlic is now available in hardy new varieties from Europe and Asia that have gardeners far from Gilroy, California (which calls itself the Garlic Capital of the World), growing their own. Planting garlic is as easy as separating a head into cloves and depositing the cloves 5 to 6 inches apart in a rich, well-drained soil and sunny location, deep enough so that the tips of the cloves are 2 inches below the surface. In colder regions, garlic is best planted in the fall; it must always be protected from freezing.

Few foods are as revered as garlic, which Homer referred to as a god. (To many a modern gourmet, it has the same status, particularly when it's homegrown.) For at least 5,000 years, garlic has been prescribed for aches and pains, colds, coughs, asthma, and bronchitis. Scientists today meet in learned congress to evaluate the pharmacological functions and nutritional benefits of eating garlic. Studies show that these benefits may include reducing the risk of developing tumors and cancers, as well as generally enhancing the immune system and protecting the body from environmental pollution.

Fight That Flu with Coneflower

Purple coneflower, *Echinacea purpurea*, is a wild North American daisy that tolerates poor or dry soil and heat far from its native woodland and prairie. Native Americans used its thick roots as a universal panacea, and early settlers followed suit.

Gardeners who value the purple coneflower for its rose-purple late-summer blossoms may be surprised to learn that the plant might offer protection against the common cold; contemporary research in Germany shows coneflower extract to be effective in boosting the immune system against both viral and bacterial infections. Purple coneflower also is a natural antibiotic that is sometimes used to treat eczema, acne, and boils.

U.S. Department of Agriculture designer-genes botanist James Duke sucked coneflower root to boost his immunity before a recent back oper-

It's the annual Gilroy Garlic Festival in Gilroy, California — with nary a werewolf in sight.

Teas and Tisanes and How to Make Them

Aside from topical applications, most medicinal uses of herbs take the form of teas — also called tisanes or decoctions. If boiling water is poured over the herb and allowed to steep and cool, the result is called an infusion or tisane. If the herb is put into the water and simmered for a while, it's a decoction. An herbal tea to drink usually pairs 1 to 3 teaspoons of dried herbs with 1 cup water, depending on personal taste and the herb's availability. A strong tea for external use can be made with up to a full ounce of fresh herbs, or half an ounce of dried, per measuring cup of water.

Make infusions of fresh flowers and leaves in small batches; they are best when fresh. Pour boiling water over the herbs in a glass, ceramic, or stainless steel container. Cover, steep for at least 10 minutes, and strain. Refrigerate any you don't use at once.

To make a decoction from bark, stems, and twigs, or from roots, bring plant parts and water to a boil in a noncorrodible pan. Reduce the heat and simmer, covered, for at least 20 minutes, then strain.

Strong teas should be drunk in small doses, perhaps a third of a cup every 2 to 3 hours, to minimize possible stomach upset.

Almost any herb can be used to make tea, but some are particularly pleasant. Peppermint makes a delicious tisane for reducing fevers, clearing the head during a cold, and preventing morning sickness. Lemon verbena tisane is a refreshing, gentle sedative that also helps settle the stomach. Use rosemary in small quantities (or combine a small sprig with lemon verbena or lemon balm) as a cure for headaches or colds and to invigorate the spirits. (In a stronger infusion, rosemary makes an antiseptic gargle for sore throats and a rinse against dandruff.) Sage is an all-around medicinal herb. An infusion may help clear a cold and reduce a fever; in a stronger brew, it makes an excellent antiseptic or a gargle for sore throats. Chamomile, as noted earlier, makes a soothing drink for ruffled nerves and at bedtime.

ation. (He claims it helped a lot.) Others turn to the herb to fend off more routine ailments. As a first line of defense against colds, flu, and sore throats, herbalists prescribe a dropperful of tincture of echinacea in water four times a day, or two capsules of the freeze-dried extract (from a health food store) at the same intervals.

Calm Down with Chamomile

Chamomile or *Anthemis*, also known as manzanilla, is another daisy grown since ancient times for flavoring and medicine. The light Spanish sherry called Manzanilla is flavored with chamomile's aromatic white flowers, so easy to cultivate that the plant is sometimes grown as a ground cover, especially in a moist climate like England's.

Chamomile is a sedative and an anti-inflammatory. A tea made from its flowers has long been used to soothe nerves and aid digestion, making it the traditional treatment for ailments not serious enough to warrant a doctor's attention. Even Peter Rabbit knew to drink a cup of chamomile tea when he was out of sorts. It's also been used for centuries to lighten and brighten hair color, relieve cramps, improve the complexion, and — in a bath — relax tired muscles.

Modern pharmacological research has confirmed the effectiveness of chamomile (particularly the variety called *Matricaria recutita*) in alleviating minor pain, cleaning wounds, killing bacteria, and treating inflammation of the skin or mouth. The tea also is used to relieve insomnia, arthritis, sciatica, colds, and fevers. Nothing is more soothing than a cup of chamomile tea, perhaps with a spoonful of honey, after a long day.

Yarrow, the Soldier's Joy

Achillea Millefolium is a common roadside herb that deserves more respect. Yarrow is native to Europe and western Asia but has naturalized in North America, New Zealand, and Australia. Common in the wild, it's also easy to grow in a sunny garden — and pretty, too, whether fresh or dried for bouquets. Legend has it that Achilles used yarrow poultices to stop the bleeding of his soldiers when they were wounded in battle— hence both its botanical name and its nickname, the military herb.

Humble, inconspicuous yarrow comes in and out of fashion. The Chinese traditionally brewed yarrow tea to treat fevers, colds, and kidney disorders. They also ate its leaves fresh in salads or dried them for snuff. The Shakers used yarrow, and so did medical personnel in battle-

PARSLEY ALL WINTER

Parsley is biennial, that is it grows from seed the first year, and blooms, ripens its seed and dies the second. It is hardy in our climate in favorable seasons and can be gathered in good condition all winter if given the protection of a frame — protection more against weather than against frost. A portable cold frame three feet wide and five and one-half feet long, or longer if more convenient, should be placed over the row in late November. If [the frame is] opened on good days to give ventilation, an abundant supply of this useful vegetable is obtained all winter. A mat thrown over the glass on cold nights helps.

—THE OLD FARMER'S ALMANAC, 1917

field hospitals during the American Civil War. Modern researchers have confirmed the observations of their wartime predecessors, crediting the tannin in the flowers and foliage of yarrow with an ability to stop bleeding, seal burns and small wounds, and act as a local antiseptic. (If you apply a poultice of yarrow, be sure to clean the wound thoroughly first.)

Yarrow contains some methyl salicylate, an analgesic, which also occurs in significant amounts in wintergreen and pennyroyal. Analgesic compounds, of which the most widely used is commercial aspirin, have a long, worldwide history of relieving pain, lowering fevers, reducing inflammation, and curing mild insomnia.

Flirt with Feverfew

Pretty daisylike feverfew, *Chrysanthemum parthenium* (also called featherfew or featherfoil), has powers that go beyond its beauty. Native to southern Europe and the Caucasus, feverfew grows well in any good garden soil or even as a houseplant. It's best propagated from seeds, which need light for germination. Although the plant will die after going to seed, the roots are perennial, and in some gardens it spreads so vigorously that it becomes invasive.

For centuries, people have used feverfew — largely externally — to treat fevers, hysteria, nervousness, and depression. In a tincture, it became an insect repellent, as a tisane it was considered both a tonic and a treatment for arthritis, and as a wash it relieved the pain of insect bites. In recent times, medical research has proved feverfew to be both an anti-inflammatory and a relaxant; scientists have demonstrated that it cures migraine headaches by relaxing the blood vessels. In studies at Chelsea College, London, 70 percent of those suffering from chronic migraines obtained relief within 6 months when they ate one to five of the bitter-tasting fresh leaves a day, most palatably included in a sandwich.

Feverfew on French, anyone?

But Don't Eat the Comfrey

Whereas traditional uses of many herbs have been supported by modern scientific research, comfrey (*Symphytum*) has fared rather badly under similar scrutiny.

Traditionally called bruisewort and knit-bone, this sturdy member of the borage family came from Europe and western Asia and naturalized in

EARTH MEDICINES

THE LORD HAS CREATED MEDICINES OUT OF THE EARTH; AND HE THAT IS WISE WILL NOT ABHOR THEM. . . . AND OF HIS WORKS THERE IS NO END.

— ECCLESIASTICUS 38:4–8

North America. Chemists note that it contains allantoin, which encourages bone, cartilage, and muscle cells to grow and speeds healing of burns and wounds.

Invasive and rejected by grazing animals, comfrey is so hard to kill that when one Catskill Mountain gardener inherited a huge patch, it took him 5 years and 5 rolls of black plastic to reclaim a garden. Comfrey enjoyed a period of wild popularity in the 1970s among back-to-the-soil

In folk medicine, comfrey baths were popular before marriage to repair the hymen and thus "restore" virginity.

MOTHER OF US ALL

GARLIC IS AS GOOD
AS HAVING TEN MOTHERS.

— OLD SAYING

gardeners. As the hippie heal-all, it was prescribed for everything from lung conditions, ulcers, broken bones, and burns to inflamed mucous membranes.

Meanwhile, back in the laboratory, research chemists were reaching disturbing conclusions about comfrey. They isolated toxins called pyrrolizidine alkaloids (PAs) in the herb, finding about ten times as much in the roots as in the leaves and sixteen times as much in young leaves as in mature leaves. Ingestion of PAs can produce a disease in which the blood vessels in the liver narrow, cutting off blood flow to and from the liver. PA poisoning was once almost unknown in this country, but recently diagnosed cases here have been attributed to eating comfrey. Although the Food and Drug Administration has yet to take formal action, herbalists should take note. Applying comfrey-leaf poultices to unbroken skin to treat burns, athlete's foot, and other skin problems may be relatively safe, but if you fancy this plant, with its large, hairy leaves and pendulous violet blossoms, you may find that its best use is as an ornamental. ☀

What Is an Herb?

Botanically, an herb is a plant — annual, biennial, or perennial — that naturally dies to the ground, having no persistent stem structure. For most gardeners, an herb is any plant grown principally for its flavor, fragrance, or medicinal properties. Practically all our native woodland plants were used as medicinal herbs by Native Americans and early settlers, and some of them adapt themselves easily to cultivation. Other herbs, wild in Asian, Indian, and other far-off gardens, are still new to many American gardeners. In learning how to grow and use all these potent and interesting plants, it may be said that today's gardeners and herbalists are still trying to catch up with their great-grandmothers.

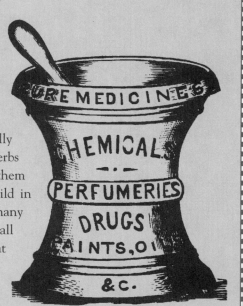

An Herb to Remember

Rosemary is the herb of friendship and fidelity; even children may know that "rosemary is for remembrance." Often included as a symbol at weddings and funerals, it's even used as an ingredient in embalming the dead — although this is where symbolism stops and practicality takes over. At this point, what embalmers remember is that the herb has a powerful disinfecting aroma.

A GARDEN TIED UP IN KNOTS

If you and your herbs like life wild, free, and unrestrained, forget about pattern gardens.

A tradition of formality in the design of herb gardens is often associated with the manors and monasteries of Europe. In fact, knot gardens date back 3,000 years to ancient Babylonia, where they were grown in intricate patterns of entwined snakes, which influenced Middle Eastern architecture and carpet design. Most gardeners have admired the neat symmetry of Italian Renaissance gardens, Tudor churchyards, and French *potagers*. Contained schemes such as these — sometimes knots, boxes, borders, or even more complicated patterns — vary a good deal in situation, planting, and focal point, but one thing they have in common is that they're rarely simple. If you want one of your own, start with pencil and paper, perennial plants, and patience.

The best plants for pattern gardens are those that are shrubby and low growing. Herbs are particularly well suited to this kind of garden because they do well in contained spaces. Both annual and perennial herbs can be raised in terra-cotta strawberry jars, then carried into the house for the winter. Herbs flourish in pots and troughs and barrels, some with pockets cut out; in wheels, using the spokes as boundaries; and in ladders laid flat on the ground.

◄

This clock, made entirely of live flowers and other growing plants, tells accurate time in a park in Edinburgh.

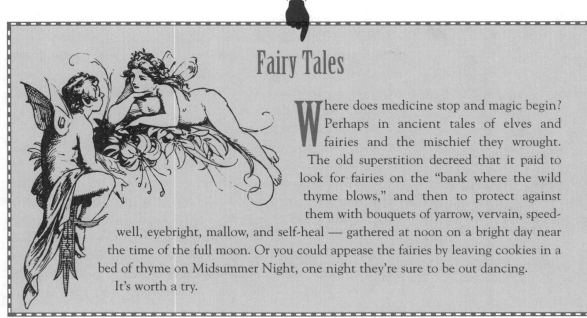

Fairy Tales

Where does medicine stop and magic begin? Perhaps in ancient tales of elves and fairies and the mischief they wrought. The old superstition decreed that it paid to look for fairies on the "bank where the wild thyme blows," and then to protect against them with bouquets of yarrow, vervain, speedwell, eyebright, mallow, and self-heal — gathered at noon on a bright day near the time of the full moon. Or you could appease the fairies by leaving cookies in a bed of thyme on Midsummer Night, one night they're sure to be out dancing.

It's worth a try.

Dressed to Kill

Some legendary herbs are extremely powerful and can be fatally poisonous. The hellebores are among these dangerous beauties, as are monkshood (aconite), foxglove, and opium poppy. (Some of these, used appropriately, play a legitimate role in modern medicine.)

Monkshood is one of the most poisonous plants found growing in the wild; its dried root is a class 1 poison. Although monkshood was once known as a sedative and painkiller, the legend behind its other name, wolfsbane, should give anyone pause. Greek hunters killed wolves, the story goes, by applying the plant's juice to their arrows.

Often the most potent herbs have bizarre flowers or seeds. Dark, helmeted monkshood is dressed to kill; thorn apple has sinister, drooping flowers and prickly pods. It's as if nature is warning us to beware, casting a spell that keeps us from harm — all part of the magic of herbs.

THE ESSENTIALS

WHERE SALT IS GOOD, SO IS
BASIL.

— ITALIAN SAYING

The rationale behind such contained beds and borders is that many culinary herbs become untidy and tangled and spread widely when left to their own devices. Confining them with stones, bricks, paths, planks, or low vegetative borders imposes limits and creates intriguing designs while keeping the plants accessible. Not that these are low-maintenance gardens. Knot and other pattern gardens require frequent, even weekly, trimming to maintain their shape.

But back to the planning. Gardeners not content with containing their gardens may be tempted to group them thematically — and few plants inspire thematic organization more than herbs. Herb lovers plant bee gardens and tea gardens, dye gardens and single-color gardens. They plant fragrance gardens and physic gardens and gardens for the birds or butterflies, wild herb gardens and gardens devoted to a single herb. Some are historically selective: biblical herb gardens and Shakespearean, of course, but also medieval, Renaissance, monastery, Victorian, colonial, and Bicentennial. Can deco and deconstructed herb gardens be far behind?

Worts Were for Women

The history of herbs (once called worts) is a history of mankind itself — or, more accurately, of womankind. Herbs have an underground history, as women do. As recently as 1920, they were often defined simply as plants grown and used by housewives. Their culture and usefulness have been a matriarchal tradition, passed down from mother to daughter and mistress to maid.

Women (and men) of every culture on every continent have used herbs as family medicines. They also have used them as teas to stimulate appetite and enhance the flavor of foods, as perfumes and deodorants to sweeten the air and help preserve linens and woolens, and as dyes for everyday and ceremonial textiles. Herbs, like women, are here to stay.

Omitted earlier in this century from private gardens in favor of showy flowers, herbs today are the subject of renewed interest among gardeners. Clearly not because of any changes in the characteristics or properties of herbs, this may be a result of a new appreciation of natural solutions or simply the recognition that in the garden the voice of experience often speaks in the idiom of old wives.

If bullets fail to stop "Them," hero James Arness
might try borage or basil, pennyroyal or lavender.

SCENTS & SENSIBILITY

An herb a day will keep pests away.

Every now and then, it seems as if insects really
enjoy playing dirty tricks on us humans. No
sooner do we find a romantic spot and spread
out the picnic than the ants launch a frontal
attack on the food, with air cover provided by black
flies and mosquitoes. So it comes as sweet revenge to
know that many aromatic herbs — scents that we
humans find most appealing — drive bugs absolute-
ly batty.

The characteristic aromas of herbs come from
the plants' release of certain organic chemicals
called terpenes, which are found in the oleoresins
and essential oils of fragrant plants. These chemicals
are volatile, evaporating quickly into the air at the

least provocation; just brushing past an aromatic herb such as thyme or rosemary will release the plant's pleasant fragrance. (People who claim to be able to "smell" an approaching storm are probably smelling the terpenes released by plants; the odor becomes more noticeable in the humid air that precedes a shower.)

Next time you go out into the woods, try an alternative to that aerosol can of bug spray you keep next to the bait box in the garage. Crush some pennyroyal leaves in a mortar and pestle, then rub the ointment into your skin. It's said to repel flies, mosquitoes, ticks, gnats, and chiggers. Inside the house, hang a swag of tansy or sage near the door to keep the flies away. Or use sachets of lavender as a pleasing and environmentally friendly alternative to mothballs. At one time or another, almost every aromatic herb has been strewn around the house as an insect repellent.

Vegetable gardeners who practice companion planting swear by culinary herbs such as basil and peppermint to ward off insect damage. And the best news of all is that these aromatic herbs don't seem to deter the beneficial bugs we do want in our gardens. Although bees tend to avoid a few repellent plants like feverfew, they are attracted to many others, such as thyme and lemon balm. Who could ask for anything more from herbs like these, which delight both humans and honeybees but give our insect enemies the willies. It's one trick that nature has played in our favor.

THE GREEN STUFF

GROW MINT IN THE GARDEN
TO ATTRACT MONEY TO
YOUR PURSE.

— OLD SAYING

Salvation Through Sage

Sage has a long history as a medicinal herb. Its genus, *Salvia*, comes from the word *salvus*, meaning "health." An old saying asks, "Why should a man die whilst sage grows in his garden?"

Tea made from sage leaves is mildly stimulating and considered a tonic. The leaves are used in cooking and in flavoring and coloring sage cheese. An old recipe for sage butter recommends mixing the smallest, youngest leaves with fresh butter, especially during the month of May.

The Essential Adelma

She's the doyenne of dill and the mentor of mints. Determined, decisive, diminutive, and delightful, Adelma Grenier Simmons is herself a force of nature. While making her home at Caprilands Herb Farm in Coventry, Connecticut, since 1929, Simmons also has made her 55-acre farm a learning center for generations of herbalists. It has been described as the best collection of herbs in the United States.

There are thirty-two herb gardens at Caprilands, some of them (Shakespearean, Victorian, and Bicentennial) inspired by history. In addition, an identification garden illustrates the herb families. Simmons not only grows herbs, knows them, and uses them for every conceivable purpose, but she also celebrates them — and life. "We celebrate constantly at Caprilands," she says, "especially everything witchy." (The mistress of Caprilands has a juniper growing by her door to ward off witches.)

The author of more than forty books on herbs, she once condensed her knowledge into six hundred words, on assignment for the *New York Times*, and produced "Herbs at a Glance," a purely practical broadsheet that has become a classic. "Anyone can grow herbs for a small family," she says, "even in a whiskey tub. Use good soil, put rosemary in the center and parsley all around with some cloves and basil."

Equally succinct are her directions for making herb vinegar: "Add plain vinegar to herbs in a bottle and let it sit for a month in the sun. That's all there is to it. You don't need a book."

Witchcraft

ONLY A WITCH CAN GROW PARSLEY.

— FINNISH SAYING

It's true that parsley seeds sometimes germinate poorly. One gardener we know has success with placing the seeds between two sheets of sandpaper and rubbing them together, then freezing them for a week. Before planting, he pours boiling water over the seeds. Does this sound like witchcraft?

To Dry or Not to Dry

Herbs dry most successfully in a dark, dry, well-ventilated place where the temperature is between 75 and 90 degrees. Most herbs dry within a week to 10 days if spread thinly on wire mesh screens or hung upside down and loosely bound in bunches. They are ready when they feel crisp to the touch but do not yet crumble. As soon as they reach this stage, remove the leaves from the stems; discard the stems and place the leaves in airtight containers; and label and date each package. To preserve color and freshness, be sure to store dried herbs away from the light.

Tender culinary herbs also freeze well. Collect herbs for freezing early in the day. You can blanch them before freezing or simply wash, dry, and package the destemmed leaves loosely in small quantities in plastic bags.

A SIMPLE SCHEME

CUT HERBS JUST AS THE
DEW DOES DRY.
TIE THEM LOOSELY AND
HANG THEM HIGH.
IF YOU PLAN TO
STORE AWAY,
STIR THE LEAVES A BIT
EACH DAY.

— AMERICAN FARMER, 1842

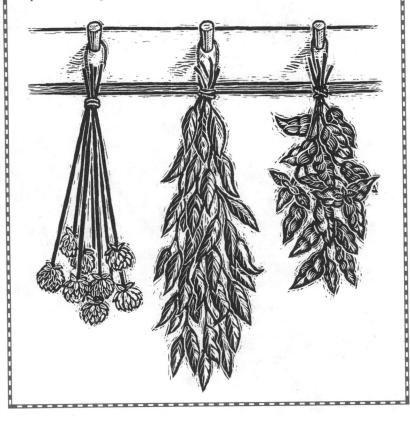

◀ Come to think of it, walnuts do resemble brains. Now that's using the old nut.

APPEARANCES CAN BE DECEIVING

If a walnut shell looked like a human brain, the theory went, perhaps it would heal a head wound.

In the Middle Ages, the Church controlled the great European centers of learning, the sciences, and many aspects of everyday life. So when it came to medicine, it only made sense that theology, not experimentation, should determine which healing herbs should be used to treat which diseases.

The system that developed has become known as the doctrine of signatures, whereby a plant's appearance or growing habit (its signature) would provide the clue as to what disease or ailment it would cure. The theory was that God had put healing plants on earth for the use of human beings and that each plant announced its healing properties to those who could read nature's

signs. Thus, a plant with heart-shaped leaves indicated that it would be effective in treating disorders of the heart.

One of the most famous champions of the doctrine of signatures was Paracelsus, a sixteenth-century German-Swiss alchemist and physician who rejected much of classical medicine in favor of herbal folk remedies. Paracelsus's given name was Philippus Aureolus Theophrastus Bombast von Hohenheim, and his middle name, together with some of his more bombastic writing, should have given sensible people pause. Yet the doctrine does have a seductive and appealing simplicity. The fact is that walnut shells *do* look something like the human brain. Who's to say that, in the absence of another cure, ground walnut shells might not work as well as anything else in dressing a head wound? More than a century after Paracelsus, the English herbalist William Coles suggested just that.

Today the doctrine of signatures remains alive only in the echoes of the names that we still use for our herbs and other plants. Latin genus names such as *Hepatica* (liverleaf) and *Pulmonaria* (lungwort) are colorful and accurate descriptions of these plants and indicate how they were once used in herbal remedies. The cure may not always have been effective, but at least it had some logic behind it.

Some theologians believed that God had provided clues to his plants' healing powers.

Herbs for Shady Spots

Not all herbs demand a full 6 hours of sun. If you want to grow herbs in a shady spot, consider Solomon's seal, bloodroot, comfrey, sweet cicely, angelica, sweet woodruff, and violet. Also shade tolerant are monkshood, chervil, feverfew, foxglove, sorrel, and valerian — as well as wintergreen and dandelion. Herbs for shade are often American natives that have immigrated from the woodland to the garden. Some of these are poisonous, however, and are best avoided if you have children. In that case, ask your local nursery to steer you toward the safer varieties.

BLIGHT

GIVE ME TRUTHS;
FOR I AM WEARY OF THE
SURFACES,
AND DIE OF INANITION.
IF I KNEW
ONLY THE HERBS AND
SIMPLES* OF THE WOOD,
RUE, CINQUEFOIL, GILL,
VERVAIN AND AGRIMONY,
BLUE-VETCH AND TRILLIUM,
HAWKWEED, SASSAFRAS,
MILKWEEDS AND MURKY
BRAKES, QUAINT PIPES AND
SUNDEW,
AND RARE AND VIRTUOUS
ROOTS, WHICH
IN THESE WOODS
DRAW UNTOLD JUICES FROM
THE COMMON EARTH,
UNTOLD, UNKNOWN, AND I
COULD SURELY SMELL
THEIR FRAGRANCE, AND
THEIR CHEMISTRY APPLY
BY SWEET AFFINITIES TO
HUMAN FLESH,
DRIVING THE FOE AND STAB-
LISHING THE FRIEND, —
O, THAT WERE MUCH, AND I
COULD BE A PART
OF THE ROUND DAY,
RELATED TO THE SUN
AND PLANTED WORLD, AND
FULL EXECUTOR
OF THEIR IMPERFECT
FUNCTIONS.

— RALPH WALDO EMERSON
*An old New England word for
medicinal herbs.

Savor the Saffron

One of the oldest cultivated plants has to be the autumn-blooming saffron (Crocus sativus). Native to the Mediterranean region, the crocus was grown thousands of years ago by ancient peoples such as the Minoans, who valued it for its beauty and usefulness.

The flavoring that we call saffron is actually the dried orange stigmas (or "threads") of the plant, which hang from the center of the flower's violet-blue petals. The ancient Greeks used these threads to dye regal robes a deep yellow. In India, saffron is still used as one of the sources for the dye that is used to dot the forehead of a wise man or pandit (from the Sanskrit word *panditah*, which is also the source of our English word *pundit*).

During the Middle Ages, the Crusaders introduced saffron to the English, who used it in a wide variety of culinary dishes. Henry VIII favored it so much in his food that he banned the use of the expensive threads as a dye in his court. Today we still use saffron — sparingly — as an ingredient in baked goods, bouillabaisse, Spanish rice, and paella.

It's fortunate that a little saffron goes a long way because it's still not cheap. Little wonder, considering that it takes roughly four thousand of the plant's blossoms to produce a single ounce of the spice.

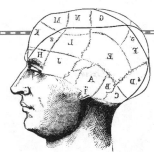

TEST YOUR HERBAL KNOWLEDGE

1 Everyone is familiar with the more common mints — peppermint, spearmint, and the like. But many other herbs also belong to the mint family (Labiatae to horticulturists). Which of the following herbs is not a member of the mint family?

a. pennyroyal
b. wintergreen
c. basil
d. rosemary

2 For countless generations, herbalists have been extracting the essences of various herbs for medicinal, culinary, and other uses. A number of techniques are used, but what do you call the process that involves soaking or fermenting the herb in alcohol?

a. an infusion
b. a decoction
c. an extract
d. a distillation

3 Match the liquor, beverage, or extract in the left-hand column with the plant in the right-hand column that is used to produce its distinctive flavor or aroma.

a. gin
b. tonic water
c. Earl Grey tea
d. May wine
e. absinthe
f. Oswego tea
g. aquavit
h. Pernod
i. angostura bitters

1. wormwood
2. gentian
3. bergamot
4. caraway
5. juniper
6. anise
7. sweet woodruff
8. cinchona
9. bee balm

---

3. a – 5; b – 8; c – 3; d – 7; e – 1; f – 9; g – 4; h – 6; i – 2.

and condensation of steam.

involves boiling the herb in water. A distillation captures the herb's essence through a process of evaporation

2. c. An infusion is created when you pour boiling water over a fresh or dried aromatic herb. A decoction

1. b.

ANSWERS

THE VEGETABLE GARDEN

"CONTRARY TO POPULAR BELIEF, IT DOES NOT COST MORE TO GROW YOUR VEGETABLES THAN TO BUY THEM. YOU CAN SPEND A LOT OF MONEY ON A VEGETABLE GARDEN BY EMPLOYING HIGH-PRICED LABOR, INVESTING IN FANCY GARDEN GADGETS, AND GOING TO EXTREMES IN PURCHASING MATERIALS. THIS WILL MAKE YOUR GARDEN A LUXURY, BUT STILL A LUXURY WORTH THE COST. ALL THIS, HOWEVER, IS A MATTER OF CHOICE, AND IS NOT NECESSARY. TO PRODUCE THE FRESH VEGETABLES WHICH ARE CONSUMED BY THE AVERAGE FAMILY ACTU-ALLY COSTS MUCH LESS THAN IT DOES TO PURCHASE THEM. YOUR OWN LEISURE HOURS CAN SUPPLY THE LABOR, AND YOU WILL FIND IT NO BURDEN; ON THE CONTRARY, THE HOURS IN YOUR GARDEN WILL BE AMONG THE PLEASANTEST OF YOUR DAY. CAREFUL TESTS HAVE SHOWN THAT IT TAKES LESS TIME TO GROW VEGETABLES IN THE HOME GARDEN THAN IT TAKES TO SHOP FOR THEM. . . .

"NO TECHNICAL EDUCATION, NO ACQUIRED MANUAL SKILLS, AND NO EXTREME PHYSICAL EXERTION ARE NEEDED. IF YOU ARE ONCE PER-SUADED TO TRY IT, YOU WILL THEREAFTER BE EXTREMELY GRATEFUL. GOOD LUCK!"

— JAMES H. BURDETT, *THE VICTORY GARDEN MANUAL*

TOP TEN TIPS FOR GREAT TOMATOES

A quick guide to growing the very best.

America's favorite backyard vegetable crop is the tomato, and with good reason. Anyone who's tasted one knows that a just-picked, sun-warmed, vine-ripened tomato is succulence itself, as far removed from a scrunched-up-in-the-package bicoastal tomato as the sun is from the moon. Because growing great tomatoes isn't hard, and because it's worth it, gardeners everywhere have given a good deal of

attention to the subject of tomato culture, and there's a lot of valuable advice going around. Our top ten tips are as good as we can make them.

1 Wait. Patience is a major ingredient in tomato success. Don't catch Tomato Fever. Don't plant seeds or set out transplants too early. Tomatoes hate cold soil, cold nights (below 55° F), and cold weather. Think tender; think tropical!

2 Select a variety of tomato that suits your climate. There are thousands of choices. Some cold-summer gardeners we know recommend Oregon Spring, Manitoba, Nepal, Sub-Arctics, and Prairie Fire; a Rhode Island seaside connoisseur plants French Lorissa (an ancient strain), Italian heirloom Costa Lutto Genovese, and Milano plum tomatoes. A water-thrifty California gardener likes Quick Pick, Sweet 100s, Taxi (the yellow one that's made for slicing), and Roma (an open-pollinated paste tomato). Burpee's Bigs, Betters, and Earlys — both the Boys and the Girls — are justly famous. The idea is to select, not settle, and to shop around. Experiment to hedge your bets, for no two seasons are the same. You'll do well to plant an early-season variety as well as mid- and late-season ones.

3 Sow your own! Every time we've had a superb tomato harvest, the plants have been started from seed (often by a friend) and transplanted into a good-size pot at an early age. Don't let the roots of seedlings touch the sides of their containers; they'll develop the best root systems if they have no limits.

4 Choose nursery seedlings carefully if you can't start your own. A good commercial grower will supply healthy 5- or 6-week-old plants, but if they're not adopted quickly and released from their root captivity, they may never recover. Be wary of peat pots. If the soil is too dry, the pots may never disintegrate. It's a good idea to release the roots from bondage, gently, just in case.

5 Enrich the soil with compost or a slow-acting general fertilizer before planting. (Use 10-50-10 in doses of about 1 tablespoon per gallon of water.) Tomatoes are heavy feeders and like fairly rich soil (but not too rich — too much nitrogen and you may not get fruit). They'll appreciate supplemental light feedings (either side dressing or foliar spray) throughout their growing season. Liquid seaweed and fish emulsion work well.

STILL GOOD ADVICE

Tomatoes should be started in the hotbed the last of March, and when two inches high, thinned out so as to be three inches apart. This gives a plant with more strength of stalk than if left to grow very close together. Set as early as possible and avoid the frost. Set the plants deep in a light, dry, and rich soil.

— *The Old Farmer's Almanac, 1896*

6 **Water as necessary to provide an even supply.** Depending on soil type and temperature, tomatoes like 1 to 1½ inches of water a week — which usually means you have to water them at least once a week. Water deeply to encourage root growth.

7 **Stake or trellis the tomato plants.** We have come around to this position gradually; we grew up believing you should let them sprawl. Staking, trellising, or using wire cages (some call them "corsets") creates a neater plant. It also takes up less space, keeps the fruit off the ground (and away from snails, slugs, and rot), and allows you to walk around the plant to pick the fruit. They say trellised tomatoes are twice as productive and also ripen faster. Live and learn.

8 **Mulch the soil around your tomato plants — but not until it has warmed up.** Use spoiled hay, black landscape fiber, composted manure, grass clippings, or anything else at hand. But do mulch — to retain the soil's moisture and keep weeds down.

Using a digital refractometer to measure the solids in your favorite tomato might just take the fun out of a BLT.

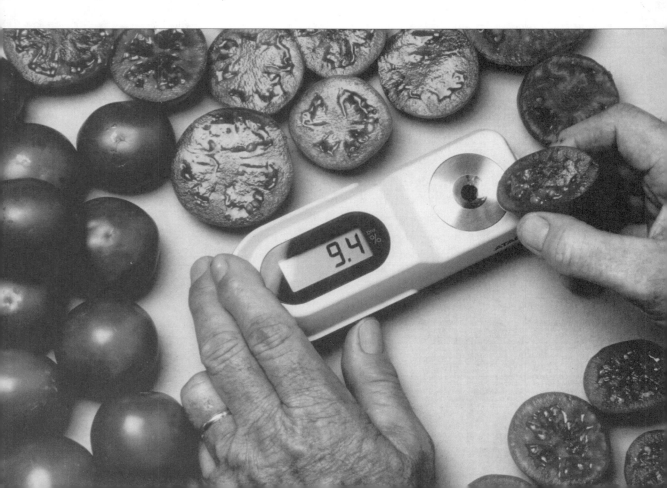

Tomato Trivia

☞ Talking to your tomato seedlings may help the outer cell layers build strength and toughen up for life in the windy world. Whistling at them is even better.

☞ A tomato contains only 35 calories. But can you eat just one?

☞ Some cherry-type tomatoes have twice the vitamin C concentration of larger tomatoes. Give 'em to the kids!

☞ Were you ever bitten by a Tomato Shark? A Tomato Shark — really a corer — is a sharp, serrated scoop that takes out the core of a tomato (with a quick bite) faster and more safely than a knife.

9 **Hasten ripening by pinching out suckers at the base of the plant and between the main stem and branches.** Prune some foliage to let in more sunlight to raise the temperature. (Temperature, not light, is what ripens tomatoes, which is why putting them on the windowsill isn't as effective as confining them in a paper bag.) Pinch off all late blossoms that will never have time to bear mature fruit. Try thermoperiodicity — chilling 1- to 1½-inch seedlings, just after their seed leaves unfold, to 50 to 55 degrees each night for a couple of weeks. This method seems to increase and hasten yields.

10 **Extend the season by pruning roots, thus encouraging a plant to send its energy aboveground for blooming.** And cover plants at night — with agricultural fleece, newspapers, sheets, plastic, or whatever's at hand — to hold in the heat of the day. Think canopies; think cloches. A New Hampshire gardener has built a full-size, plastic-walled tomato shed to coddle his crop.

Or try this: just before the killing frost, carefully harvest whole vines with the immature fruit and hang them in a cool place. They are beautiful and ripen gradually. We hung ours in the dining room one year, providing diners with tomatoes for the picking within arm's reach. ✺

GREENS FOR THE TABLE

WHO WANTS TO EAT A GOOD SUPPER SHOULD EAT A WEED OF EVERY KIND.

— OLD ITALIAN SAYING

What's a Vermont garden — or a Saturday night supper — without beans?

SPILLING THE BEANS ABOUT VERMONTERS

Beans are cheap. Self-sufficient. Capable of thriving in tough climates. A lot like Vermonters . . .

There is an association between beans and the state of Vermont that's hard to pin down but undeniable.

Since the days of the earliest settlers, beans have been an important food crop for Vermonters. The Green Mountain State has some of the best soil in northern New England — thanks to the late, great glacier— and has always bred farmers. Thrifty Vermont farmers grew a lot of seed stock, and beans are especially well suited to the climate.

Some years beans are about the only crop Vermont gardeners can count on. "I always figure that when I plant beans, the garden pays for itself," one western Vermont gardener volunteered. "I struggle with the other crops, but the beans come through."

"My husband's parents raised six or more varieties of beans," a Benson, Vermont, gardener told us. "During the Depression, they sold them for five cents a pound. Every year, they'd save them in a box, and what was was left over in the spring, you planted. Years ago, everyone saved beans. People more or less had to look out for themselves."

Just about as self-sufficient as the average Vermonter, beans are largely self-pollinating and can be saved without much difficulty, even in a cold climate. All over the state, gardeners years ago took to saving their own bean seeds — beans peculiar to a single family or neighborhood and handed down from one generation to the next.

Many of these heirloom beans, some under cultivation for more than a hundred years now, are known by family names. The list of varieties reads like a hill-town tax roster: Kimball, Spencer, Perry, Mrs. Somer's, McCaslan Pole Beans, Steuben Yellow Eyes, Johnson, and Jacob's Cattle.

For a fix on these Vermont beans and many others, try the Vermont Bean Seed Company in Hubbardton. When it was founded in 1974, the company sold only beans — thirty varieties, to be exact, listed on a single typed sheet. Now its plump catalog purveys some eighty-nine varieties of beans and much more.

Beanpoles, bean pots, bean suppers. According to our source, the very best bean suppers in the Green Mountain State are held in the little town of Brownsville. Try the baked beans with brown bread and piccalilli. If you're lucky, the bean pot will hold the local wine-striped Cranberry beans.

If you don't know the Vermont Cranberry bean, you don't know beans about Vermont. ☀

ADVICE FOR POTATO PICKERS

Never commence harvesting your potatoes till they have come to full maturity, or till the frost has killed the tops down. While the tops are green, the bulbs are growing and improving. In digging them, use either the plow or the potato hook. As soon as they are out of the ground, let them be picked up. Never permit them to remain out in the sun or air longer than you can possibly help. Every attentive observer has noticed that potatoes are of the best flavor and quality after they have come to maturity and while they are still in the ground. The longer they are dug and exposed to light and air, the more of this fine flavor is gone, till it is wholly lost and they become unpalatable and unwholesome. Potatoes that remain all winter in the earth where they grew, are in excellent condition for the table in the spring.

— *The Old Farmer's Almanac, 1842*

A Harvesting Tip from Great-Aunt Martha

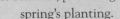

On May 9, 1809, Martha Ballard "sett Turnips & Cabbage stumps" in her garden in Hallowell, Maine. Another year, she set cabbage stumps on April 18 — 165 of them in all. In 1806, she planted on May 4 and had a harvest 2 weeks later, mixing the fresh shoots with wild greens harvested from the fields and forest.

This we know from Martha's diary, *A Midwife's Tale: The Life of Martha Ballard, Based on Her Diary, 1785 – 1812* (by Laurel Thatcher Ulrich, published by Knopf in 1990 and winner of a Pulitzer Prize in 1991). The diary reminds us of an almost-forgotten garden trick, as simple as it is thrifty.

When nineteenth-century gardeners like Martha Ballard harvested their cabbages and turnips in the fall, they uprooted them entirely — stems, heads, and roots — and kept the whole plants in the root cellar for the winter. As soon as the ground could be worked in the spring, these gardeners planted the roots (the heads had long since been eaten, of course) in the cool soil. Soon they harvested bushy fresh green sprouts — a tasty addition to soups, salads, or fricasees at a time when the rest of the garden was just beginning to be planted.

The wintered-over mother plants didn't develop into mature vegetables but went to seed by the end of the summer, providing ample seeds for the next spring's planting.

Bringing the idea into the twentieth century, four-season gardener Eliot Coleman suggests that you don't have to wait until spring to enjoy the fresh greens. In December or January, try sprouting winter-stored beets, celeriac, rutabagas, parsley, or cabbage. Coleman does this in sand on a windowsill, keeping the roots damp. The reward: the perfect flavorful garnish to set off many a midwinter dish.

WHAT DEER WON'T EAT

Is there anything edible that a deer won't devour for dinner?

Some people will grow to great lengths to keep the deer out of the corn crop.

The facts are plain.

Nothing.

There is virtually nothing edible that a hungry deer will not eat. Deer eat the twigs and bark of trees and shrubs and devour fruits, vegetables, and flowers.

But take heart. Deer do have preferences. Like most vegetarians, they have their favorite foods — which may, in fact, be some of *your* favorite foods — and they turn up their noses at others.

Deer do find a few things distasteful. Most of these are characterized by strong (the stronger the better) smells or prickles. Deer have sensitive nostrils that recoil at the pungent scents of mints, yarrows, and lantanas, among herbal offerings. Alliums and other members of the onion family seem to repel them. And sure enough, they know well which plants are

poisonous — monkshood, baneberry, rhubarb leaves, narcissuses, colchicums, hellebores, and poison ivy, among others — and don't deign to dine on those. Mustard greens and peppery cresses don't suit discriminating deer; junipers and roses are usually too scratchy; and plants with dense, woolly foliage, such as lamb's ears and thistles, are generally avoided, although not always.

Researchers at the Universities of Georgia and California have compiled a list of deer-resistant plants that includes butterfly bush, box-woods, calendula, chrysanthemums, brooms, kerria, mahonias, nandina, rhododendrons, oleander, tulips, and daffodils. Other observers might add peonies, astilbes, irises, and lady's-mantle.

Some gardeners put a lot of effort and imagination into deer deterrents, which are sometimes successful and sometimes not. Barricades are worth a try: some deer don't like to climb steps or wander through netting or narrow passages between structures. Some gardeners swear by soap — specifically perfumed soap of the sort found in hotel rooms —hanging it on the branches of fruit trees or placing it in slit plastic bags left between garden rows. Others recommend human hair, scattered or hung in stockings; urine; egg whites; or lion dung. (Some deterrents are more readily available than others.) Gardeners have been known to install night-lights, radios, or noisemakers or to erect scarecrows.

Commercial animal repellents are a possibility — if you're willing to shop and spray. A repellent called Hinder works well in the spring; later, Ro-Pel seems to be more effective. But chemical repellents work only in the exact spots where applied, and it's tough to spray every inch of a large yard and garden.

A good dog can surely inhibit the activities of visiting deer, but a good dog is hard to find. (Most dogs we know like to spend the night in or under the bed, and cats are no use at all in this respect.)

All in all, when the time comes that you're fed up with feeding the deer, build a good fence. ☀

Another Theory Shot Down

Folk wisdom holds that bars of smelly soap or scatterings of human hair will keep deer out of a garden. But the Louisiana Cooperative Extension Service has shed new light on this theory. Using two separate garden plots, they placed human hair in one and political signs left over from a recent election in the other. The signs proved more effective than the hair.

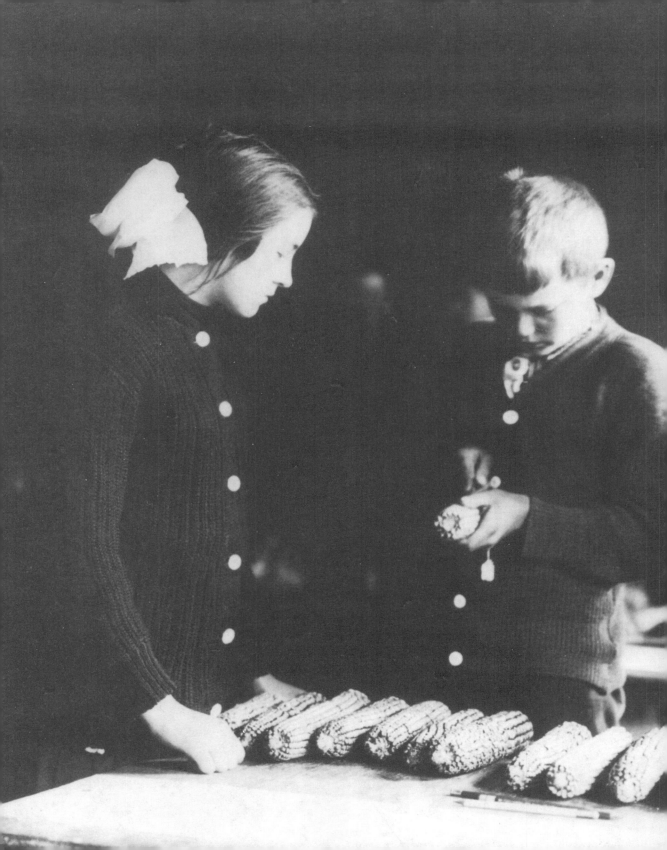

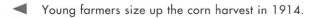
Young farmers size up the corn harvest in 1914.

THE VEGETABLE THAT CAN'T SURVIVE WITHOUT US

It's an amazing plant, corn. It just can't live alone.

Corn. It's beautiful; it's nutritious; it's the most important crop in the United States — and it needs us.

The dependency is our own fault. American farmers and corn breeders have fiddled with this poor plant until it can no longer survive in the wild. A modern ear of corn enclosed in its husks, you see, is unique in the plant kingdom; it lacks a mechanism for dispersing its seeds. In nature, it has a low survival rate. When an ear of corn drops to the ground and finds conditions suitable for germination, countless seedlings emerge — creating such fierce competition for moisture and nutrients that all usually die before they reach the reproductive stage.

Which is where we come in. Human hands, of course, can easily disperse seed kernels in a deliberate pattern, setting them deep enough and far enough apart to foster successful growth. Under our protection, corn can and has thrived as a garden and field crop. And if corn needs us, we have to admit that we're undeniably codependent.

Today we consume very small amounts of corn directly — as corn on the cob, breakfast cereals, Indian pudding, polenta, and occasionally bourbon. But more than three-quarters of our corn crop is consumed by animals and transformed into meat, milk, eggs, and other animal products. This is what makes corn our basic food plant, just as it was for the original settlers of this hemisphere. No wonder it has been proposed that an ear of corn replace the eagle as our national symbol. After all, though it's not exactly an independent creature of the wild, corn does have a few other things going for it. Consider . . .

The Amazing Grain

☞ By 1492, Native Americans were growing roughly 50,000 acres of corn each year in river valleys and mountain coves.

☞ Nearly 100 percent of the corn grown today by farmers in the Midwest is hybrid, a modern seed corn developed since 1926.

☞ Corn is the most efficient plant we have for capturing the energy of the sun and converting it into food.

☞ Corn is planted on more acres than any other American crop, and each year the corn harvested in the United States is worth more than any other crop.

☞ Like all grains, corn is a grass.

☞ Corn has the strongest roots of any annual, reaching down as far as 7 feet and out 3 to 4 feet.

☞ While the roots are reaching into the soil for nutrients, the leaves of the cornstalk unfold one by one, alternating between opposite sides of the stalk.

☞ At the same time, the leaf sheaths that surround the stalk also alternate in the way their margins overlap. Half of them overlap from left to right, as a man's shirt buttons; half overlap from right to left, as a woman's blouse fastens.

☞ A stalk of corn has been known to grow 8 inches in 24 hours.

☞ The average ear of corn has about 800 kernels.

☞ Researchers have estimated that a single vigorous corn plant produces between 30 and 60 million individual pollen grains, or roughly 25,000 to 30,000 for every future kernel (seed) of corn.

☞ One scientist has calculated that a typical Nebraska corn field produces some 42,500 pollen grains per square inch. And that's nothing to sneeze at. ☀

KEEP PLANTING!

To have sweet corn every day until frost comes, begin early in the season and plant a row every two weeks until the Fourth of July.

— *The Old Farmer's Almanac, 1896*

Wanna Bet?

Have you ever found an ear of corn with an odd number of rows? Bet you can't do it! A single ear can contain from eight to thirty rows, but the number is almost always even.

Hey, who's counting?

An early researcher defends the goodness of greens.

▼

GOURMET WEEDS

When is a weed not a weed?
When it's a salad.

Country folk have known for years that some of the peskiest, most common weed-like greens actually taste pretty darned good. Now it turns out that they're good for you, too— and you can't beat the price. (How did something so easy ever get to be au courant?) Before you turn up your nose at Purslane Salad or Lamb's Quarters Soup, remember that the country folk just might be on to something.

Purslane

To say that purslane is easy to grow is to understate the case. It's rampant. A World War II victory garden manual called it "America's worst weed." But researchers say that purslane leaves, which have a mild nutty flavor, provide more of the desirable omega-3 fatty acids than any other vegetable source.

Old farmers called purslane (*Portulaca oleracea*) pusley. Our forebears didn't hesitate to eat it when they found this European transplant growing wild, but the notion of actually cultivating the plant has been remarkably slow to catch on among American gardeners. A hot-weather green, purslane prefers fertile garden soil, but like any weed deserving the name, it will survive in almost any soil. Snip off its plump, shiny leaves and stems whenever you want to fill your salad plate and encourage new plant growth. Cultivated purslane (*Portulaca oleracea sativa*) is more erect than the wild variety and has larger, meatier leaves of a bright golden green. (Cultivated purslane is actually a different variety from the wild plant. Like most cultivated varieties, it's better.)

Lamb's Quarters

Lamb's quarters (*Chenopodium album*), commonly called pigweed, love to take root in compost and manure piles, sending a taproot deep in search of quality nutrients. No wonder, then, that lamb's quarters are nutritious — high in iron, calcium, albumin, and vitamins A and C. Lamb's quarters are even more nutritious than spinach, which they resemble in taste.

Some people think that lamb's quarters taste better than spinach. The gray-green leaves with dusty silver backs are less acrid and have a tender, melting texture. Harvest them young, before they reach 10 inches in length, rinse them thoroughly, and eat them raw with olive oil and garlic. Or cook them in salted water for 7 to 10 minutes. They are delicious topped with butter or included in an omelet or soup — anywhere spinach might go. Some cooks blanch and freeze lamb's quarters to eat all winter.

One variety, Giant Lamb's Quarters, also known as Mountain Spinach or Orach, is both ornamental and colossal. It grows nearly 5 feet tall with a very large leaf — as large as that of collard greens. Very sweet in taste, it thrives from the equator to the Arctic.

If your garden gives you these fine-flavored weeds, count yourself fortunate. And the next time a neighbor laughs at all your "weeds," invite her over for dinner.

Note: Should you decide to try either purslane or lamb's quarters, be sure you do not harvest plants that have been subjected to pesticides or any other chemical contaminant. And be careful to wash all greens well in several changes of water. Nothing is nastier than a mouthful of grit in the salad. ☀

GETTING RID OF WEEDS

Weeds can be raised cheaper than most other crops, because they will bear more neglect. But they don't pay in the end. They are the little vices that beset plant life, and are to be got rid of the best way we know how. The first thing is to avoid getting their seeds into manure. It is almost as important to keep the manure, as to keep the land, clean. The next is to take them early. It is cheaper to nip them in the bud than to pull them up, root and branch, when they get ahead. Here is where the brainwork comes in. It is work that must be done.

— *The Old Farmer's Almanac, 1881*

SCARE THE CROWS, AMUSE THE NEIGHBORS

Sometimes the oldest ideas are the best ones.

Gardeners have been setting up scarecrows since crows learned to steal seeds, and still do — because they work. Motion is the key, and noise helps, but there are no absolute rules when it comes to the Art of the Scarecrow.

Most scarecrows suggest the human figure — tall or short, fierce or funny. For a basic garden guardian, start with a post (or branch or broom handle) about 6 feet long and fit one leg of a pair of old pants through it, leaving the other leg free. Pound the post into the ground, and wire or nail a crosspiece at about shoulder height. Then put on a shirt with sleeves, loose and long enough to flop off the ends of the shoulders, and add a head.

A gallon milk jug makes a good head, about the right size to wear a hat. So does a basin, an oilcan, a basket, or even a mop head. Add a face if you fancy, or a Halloween mask, hat, bandanna, tangle of rope, or scarf. This is the time to get whimsical: you can build a creature out of found objects from a yard sale, your attic, or even the town dump.

Anything that moves or sparkles is good. Deck out your scarecrow with a bit of tinsel or a junk-jewelry chain, dangle aluminum pie plates cut into fingers, or go for realism. One gardener who found a department store mannequin and dressed it in her own clothes got a reputation for haughtiness because it didn't wave back at passing neighbors.

Responding to a serious deer problem, a California gardener set up a really threatening "scaredeer" made to look like a 6-foot, 200-pound patrolman. It scared the deer for 4 days; on the fifth day, a doe was seen using the effigy as a back scratcher.

One of the most impressive scarecrows we've seen is a massive, hay-stuffed effigy of the influential British garden designer Gertrude Jekyll (a.k.a. Saint Gertrude) at Stonecrop Gardens in Cold Spring, New York. Bespectacled and broad of shoulder, gauzy Saint Gertrude has a powerful presence — especially, according to Caroline Burgess, Stonecrop's director, when there's a misty twilight. ☀

GIVE YOUR PLANTS A GOOD (STIFF) DRINK
Can it be that plants actually respond better to alcohol than to water?

GREAT DRINKER

If you try to raise celery, give it plenty of water. It is a great drinker, and, if it hasn't enough to quench its thirst, it is apt to grow tough and hollow. Keep the plants growing right along from the time they appear aboveground in the seedbed till they are transplanted to rich soil, and water as often as they need it, and you'll have it plump and tender.

— *The Old Farmer's Almanac, 1886*

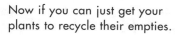

Now if you can just get your plants to recycle their empties.

Every gardener knows this familiar scene. You walk out to the vegetable garden at the end of a hot summer day. The leaves on the tomatoes are drooping; the soil is dry and dusty. You can almost hear the plants whispering, "Water, water," like some French legionnaire crossing the Sahara. You go for the garden hose and begin giving your crops a good drink of water.

That's all well and good, but if the results of recent research are any indication, your vegetables may really be asking not for plain old water, but for a highball.

In field experiments conducted in Arizona by Arthur Nonomura and Andrew Benson, the *New York Times* reported in 1992, crops that were sprayed with diluted methanol (wood alcohol) produced significantly greater yields than plants sprayed with water. What's more, the crops sprayed with the alcohol solution actually required less watering than the control plants.

Among their astonishing results, the two researchers found that when they sprayed plants with diluted methanol, cabbages doubled in size, tomatoes grew faster and tasted sweeter, roses produced more flowers, and fruits as diverse as strawberries and watermelons had better yields.

Exactly how methanol benefits these plants remains a mystery, although it may act to inhibit a process known as photorespiration, in which plants lose much of the solar energy that they capture through photosynthesis. It is thought that the methanol spray makes the plants more efficient, enabling them to retain more of the energy they receive from the sun and turn it into new growth.

Don't start sprinkling vodka over your tomatoes just yet, though. Researchers still have a long way to go to learn exactly which plants enjoy an occasional snort and which are confirmed teetotalers. Methanol in a concentrated form can be toxic to plants, and some crops such as corn and sorghum (which are already very energy efficient) don't seem to benefit at all from the methanol treatment. The amount of sunlight a crop receives also may determine how much it will benefit from an alcohol spray.

On the other hand, don't be surprised if, sometime in the near future when you go out to the garden, you hear your thirsty plants talking to you again — this time singing a barbershop chorus of "How Dry I Am." ☀

We're Waiting for the Calvin Coolidge Cucumber

S everal years ago, Rick Tweddell of Cincinnati, Ohio, was working for a toy company when he had an inspired idea. Why not sell plastic molds to gardeners so that they could place the molds around their vegetables and grow different designer shapes — hearts or diamonds or even living veggie profiles of friends or famous people?

Tweddell loved the idea, but his bosses hated it, so Tweddell began producing and marketing his Vegiform molds himself. For the gardener, there's no real trick to growing molded produce; anyone who can grow cucumbers, melons, or squash can grow something that looks like a Garden Elf ("Our most popular mold," Tweddell says, "and it works very well with an eggplant") or a U.S. president.

Most Vegiforms are two-piece plastic molds that a gardener fastens around a growing vegetable. After that, Mother Nature does all the work. In about a week's time, the vegetable fills out and takes the shape of the Vegiform design, and the mold can be removed.

About 95 percent of Vegiform molds are sold through catalogs, at prices ranging from $10.95 to $14.95, although Tweddell ("for a really exorbitant price") will design and even grow "vanity vegetables" in the spitting image of anyone you might wish to immortalize. For a mere $2,500, you receive a bust of the subject, half a dozen Vegiform custom molds, and a supply of vegetables grown in that lucky person's likeness. "You can have a bushel of your buddy," Tweddell says. What better gift for the gardener who has everything?

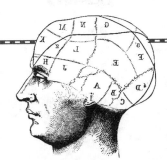

TEST YOUR VEGETABLE KNOWLEDGE

1 Which of the following vegetables is not a member of the mustard family (Cruciferae)?

a. arugula
b. Brussels sprouts
c. horseradish
d. okra
e. rutabaga

2 What is the more commonly used name for the root vegetable known as "oyster plant"?

3 Based on the descriptions and ingredients listed below, name each of the following popular vegetable dishes.

a. a Native American dish mixing beans and corn
b. a garlicky eggplant dip from the Middle East made with tahini (pureed sesame seeds)
c. a cold Spanish soup made with tomatoes, cucumbers, and other vegetables
d. a Sicilian vegetable relish or appetizer made with eggplant, celery, tomatoes, and capers

ANSWERS
1. d. Okra is a member of the mallow family, or Malvaceae. 2. salsify.
3. a – succotash; b – baba ganouj; c – gazpacho; d – caponata.

CHAPTER EIGHT

THE HARVEST

"AUTUMN IS THE BEST SEASON IN WHICH TO SNIFF, AND TO SNIFF FOR PLEASURE, FOR THIS IS THE SEASON OF UNIVERSAL PUNGENCY. THE ODORS OF AUTUMN, INDEED, LARGELY CONSTITUTE IT FOR US FROM YEAR TO YEAR, ODORS WITH THEIR STRANGE POWER TO EVOKE MEMORIES MORE THAN SIGHTS OR SOUNDS DO. IN THE HOUSE, FRA-GRANCE OF STORED APPLES, OF SPICY PICKLING AND FRUITY PRESERV-ING, OF HERBS HUNG UP TO DRY, OF TURPENTINEY BALSAM NEEDLES AND MEADOWY EVERLASTING FLOWERS IN FRESH-MADE PILLOWS; AND OUTDOORS, THE SMELLS OF MOLDY LEAVES, OF LEAVES BURNING IN AROMATIC BONFIRES, OF ACRID CHIMNEY SMOKE FALLING TO THE GROUND BEFORE A MIZZLING RAIN, OF DAMP EARTH. . . .

"AT THE WIDE BENCHES JUST INSIDE THE BARN DOORS I BEGIN TO PEEL AND SLICE AND CHOP, GETTING READY FOR PICKLING AND CANNING. EVERY DAY MORE AND MORE FILLED CROCKS AND JARS CROWD THE BUTT'RY SHELVES. THE KITCHEN SMELLS AS IF THE SPICE ARGOSIES WHICH SAILED FROM THE ORIENT FOR QUEEN ELIZABETH WERE ANCHORED HERE, CINNAMON, GINGER, PEPPER AND CLOVE. JELLIES PURPLE AND AMBER AND RED ARE SET TO CLEAR ON LITTLE SHELVES ACROSS THE KITCHEN WINDOWS, AND THE SUNLIGHT SHINES THROUGH AND MAKES THEM GLOW LIKE STAINED GLASS."

— BERTHA DAMON, *A SENSE OF HUMUS*

FIRST FRUITS

For the impatient gardener, the pick of the fast-growing vegetable varieties.

Patience is a virtue, but it's a virtue tested by gardeners who are anxious to get their vegetables out of the garden and onto the table as quickly as possible. Some of these gardeners are driven less by their taste buds than by a fierce competitive urge to have the earliest peas, tomatoes, or sweet corn in the county.

Trying to one-up your gardening neighbors is a long-standing tradition. Thomas Jefferson used to have a running bet with his neighbor as to who would harvest the first peas each year. The deal was that the winner would invite the loser over for dinner and serve him the first peas of the season.

In the following list, we've selected a few of the extra-early varieties for some competitive crops, just to give you a leg up on your neighbors next year. The number of days to maturity is approximate, of course, and refers to the time from direct-seeding or from transplanting, depending on the crop. None of the following varieties are hybrids, which are sometimes bred to mature even earlier than these standard strains. Who knows, someday we may have a tomato that goes from seed to ripe fruit in less than a week. Then again, that would take all the fun out of growing the first beefsteaks on the block.

Cucumbers

Straight 8	52 days

Eggplant

Applegreen	62 days
Early Black Egg	65 days

Green Snap Beans, Bush

Earliserve	41 – 47 days
Prelude	45 days
Remus	40 – 48 days
Spring Green	41 days

◄ Sometimes the abundance of the harvest is sobering to consider.

Muskmelons

Midget	60 days
Montana Gold	60 days

Peas, Fresh Shelling

Alaska	50 – 60 days
Early May	55 days
Pacemaker	55 – 58 days

Sweet Bell Peppers

King of the North	57 – 65 days
Merrimack Wonder	60 days

Sweet Corn

Fisher's Earliest	60 days
Glacier	65 days
Honey Cream	60 days
Simonet	58 days

Tomatoes

Oregon Spring	55 days
Shoshone	49 days
Siberia	40 – 60 days
Sub-Arctic Plenty	40 – 59 days
Swift	54 days
Tigerella	55 – 56 days

Watermelon

Early Midget	68 days
Garden Baby	68 – 78 days
New Hampshire Midget	65 – 82 days
Northern Sweet	68 – 75 days

Saving the Seeds of Your Favorite Tomatoes

I n tomatoes, as in courtship, there's no accounting for taste. Some like 'em tangy; some like 'em sweet. If you're like the rest of us, somewhere along the line you've tasted a tomato you thought sublime. The best way to have your favorite on demand is to save its seeds. Tomato seeds aren't hard to collect and store (they're viable for up to 4 years), as anyone who's seen volunteers in the compost pile knows.

Fermenting tomato seeds for a few days kills any diseases they may be carrying. Just put a squashed tomato in a glass, add water to cover, and set the glass in a spot where you'll remember to keep an eye on it. (A kitchen shelf is usually good.)

Stir the brew at least once a day for 3 to 4 days. It will begin to bubble on the second or third day, depending on the temperature of the room. On the fourth or fifth day, you'll be able to see floating pulp and weak seeds floating on the surface. Spoon these off, then strain, rinse, and dry the heavy seeds that have sunk to the bottom.

Label the seeds and store them in a cool, dry place until it's time to start them — about 5 weeks before transplant time.

TRICKS AND TRADITIONS FOR EXTENDING THE SEASON

To everything there is a season . . . but some seasons are too short.

Most gardeners would trade a hothouse for a longer growing season, and most have a scheme or two for extending the harvest past the first light frosts of fall. In this pursuit, sometimes the old-timers' tricks are the most successful ones. Herewith, our best schemes.

Add Stones to the Garden

In the old days, farmers planted tomato vines on the south sides of the stone walls that edged their fields. The trick made sense; stones gather and store heat during the day and release it at night. The modern gardener, lacking a stone wall, is likely to have good luck ringing a tomato plant with a circle of rocks, close to but not touching the plant's stem. Add stones to the protective wall as the plant grows. They moderate temperature changes, encourage root growth, prevent the invasion of weeds, and help keep the soil moist.

Protect with a Porta-Frame

Early American gardeners built frames of thin boards set with panes of glass. These structures protected plants from early frosts (and late-spring ones) by raising the temperature and reducing the wind chill. It's the greenhouse effect, made portable. In fact, some of the nineteenth-century frames were even styled with beveled sides so that they could be

Rocks like these at Stonehenge would coddle more than a few tomatoes.

stacked for easier storage.

Today's cutting-edge gardeners use very similar devices, often with sturdy wooden frames and plastic covers. Light-weight and easily moved, they're a clear improvement on the Victorian's heavy glass cloches.

Install a Magic Box

Gardeners who find portable frames useful might take to another season stretcher common in old-fashioned kitchen gardens: the cold frame. The idea is older than glass — cold frames used to be fitted with mica — and perfectly simple.

In its purest form, a cold frame is a bottomless box covered with a lid that admits light. The angled lid catches the sun; the frame magnifies the sun's warmth and shelters tender plants. A cold frame can extend the growing season at least a month in the fall.

Old-fashioned brick or stone cold frames, built with heavy glass that cracked easily, were the workhorses of the Victorian garden. Modern versions are usually lighter in weight and may use shatter- and ultraviolet-resistant plastic instead of glass; some even fold flat for storage. On very cold nights, give your miniature greenhouse extra protection by banking the frame with leaves, straw, or hay and insulating the top (where heat most readily escapes) with old blankets, straw, or whatever else is at hand.

The simplicity of cold frame construction seems to stimulate creativity. We've had great luck with impromptu cold frames constructed of cast-off storm windows hinged to the south side of the house. A neighbor took an even more casual approach: she set up a barricade of hay bales and topped it with a sheet of fiberglass. It worked just fine. ☀

THE PANTRY OF MY DREAMS
A fantasy of a different sort.

Some women dream of passion, of pearls and Paris fashion. My dreams are of another sort of perfection, expressed in shelves and cupboards, drawers and bins and baskets. I want a pantry just like the one my grandmother used to have.

The perfect pantry — can you see it in your mind's eye?

It's a small, airy room of the sort Yankees used to call a buttery. Opening off the kitchen, it's a serene retreat — small and snug, fitted with a door, preferably facing north for coolness and big enough to allow for a tall window to shed natural light and provide ventilation. Floor-to-ceiling shelves offer reassuring storage space, providing for plenty.

There's a place for everything. High shelves lined with carefully cut newspaper house seldom-used dishes and equipment — the eggnog bowl and cups, the huge Adamsware turkey platter and plates, the meat grinder, fluted tin molds for steamed puddings, trays standing on end. A wide, waist-high counter built in a U-shape around the room provides extra workspace, even a place to eat a little meal, perched on the wooden step-seat, while watching birds in the backyard grapevines.

The counter space under the window, covered with a smooth, easily cleaned sheet of linoleum, is perfect for rolling out cookies or pastry; bins of flour and sugar are handy, and cookie cutters are piled in the nearest drawer. Ceiling hooks dangle hams, herbs, braids of garlic, and onions. And behind doors in the cool lower cupboards, baskets and barrels shelter squashes, more onions, potatoes, apples, and reserves of flour for baking bread.

One whole wall of this platonic pantry is devoted to canning equipment. Those of us without ideal pantries can surely testify that canning gear is always either in the way or impossible to find. Here, in the canning cupboard, all those odd little jars — the ones that turn up on counters and shelves and gather under the sink — keep company. Jar rings, funnels, strainers, and paraffin sit neatly in a drawer, awaiting jelly-making time. Black enamel canning kettles rest on the lower shelves.

What would an analyst make of my craving for this compartmentalized cupboard? It's easy to see a desire for order; a need to have favorite tools and possessions nearby but contained by the pantry door; an ancient comfort in knowing food is safely stored, the lullaby of the larder. All this, perhaps, plus nostalgia for a sweet-spicy–smelling old-fashioned pantry with a pie or two cooling on the counter.

Ah, wouldn't it be wonderful?

◀ A wealth of preserves and pickles in the pluperfect pantry.

THE COMPULSION TO CAN

What demon drives us to this labor-intensive autumn ritual?

If you can, you know what I mean. Canning is more than a tradition. It's a seasonal compulsion, practically a reflex action, as irresistible as skipping in springtime or barbecuing on the Fourth of July.

It may not even make economic sense. Canned tomatoes are readily available in markets — sometimes at a price that makes us marvel, knowing the labor involved between the seed and the supermarket. It's not the money saved.

Partly, it's the flavor. Store-bought tomatoes will do in a pinch, but nothing beats home-canned tomatoes for taste, much less for a sense of accomplishment and seasonal security. "Can the best, eat the rest," the old-timers said. Nothing is prettier to look at than red, red tomatoes behind glass; nothing brings back stronger memories of summer.

Certainly, in my case, it's a family tradition. My mother always canned tomatoes, and she taught me the cold-pack, hot-juice method. (Thirty years without a single case of botulism.) Over the years, I always set time aside to join her in the annual skin-off, boil-down, and jar-up. You might call it a female bonding ritual. My father stayed out of the way until it was time to lift the wire racks, heavy with quart jars, out of the boiling kettle.

I don't know many men who can tomatoes, although one who does has built an outdoor canning kitchen in his back yard. There he processes his tomatoes over a wood fire, picnic table nearby for counter space, only feet from the garden where he grows them. In contrast, putting by for winter is a seasonal rite for a good many women who seem possessed by a passion to process and preserve. I have a neighbor who hates tomatoes and won't eat them in any form, yet she has been known to boil up quarts of tomato sauce. Another neighbor eagerly bought and canned two bushels of tasteless, truck-weary California tomatoes the June she was newly married.

It's hard to hold off when you're dazzled by all those empty jars, but if you live in a northern climate, wait you must. It's early fall before New England tomatoes come into season. Wait a little longer — by October you can pick up cheap "canning tomatoes" at local farms. They're the ones I like best: dead ripe with insignificant blemishes. Their presence on the kitchen table can spark a frenzy of canning. (Plum tomatoes, a.k.a. pasta tomatoes, are flavorful and low in moisture, making them perfect for sauce.) Don't lose your head at the roadside stand, though; one bushel is plenty to can —in addition, perhaps, to your own backyard harvest.

At least it's plenty in terms of the work involved. No matter how many tomatoes I can, it's never too many to eat. There may be beets or applesauce left on the cellar shelves at the end of the winter, but there are never left-over tomatoes. My friend Bob's Italian mother used to can exactly fifty-two quarts, one for each Sunday's spaghetti sauce. I could never be so systematic, but I can all I can.

So now's the time. Give in to it; it's part of the fall nesting frenzy. Find the huge enamel canning kettle that gets in the way the rest of the year. Trudge down into the cellar and lug up those boxes of jars. Buy new lids or rubber rings. Choose a good day and take a deep breath. There's no point in fighting the survival instinct.

The passion to preserve — be it the species or the tomato crop — seems to be a particularly feminine trait.

▼

◀ Get serious; don't proffer — deliver!

GETTING BEYOND GARDEN GUILT

How to face your fears and toss the last of the tomatoes.

The harvest garden can be too much of a good thing.

Back in May, the temptation to sow a few more rows of seeds was irresistible. Back in July, it seemed too cruel to uproot any of those plucky little plants — they were all doing so well. How could you choose where to discriminate, which to murder?

Now it's harvest time — the full, fat time of year — and everything has ripened at once. The very word *zucchini* has become a joke. You're hit with a deluge of cucumbers and a blizzard of beans. Bushels of tomatoes are bursting on browning vines. The unspoken cry, "Use me or lose me," is in the air, thick as pollen in May.

Turning a deaf ear is not easy for any gardener — he (or she) who knows what went into producing this bounty, fears the terrible touch of frost, and lives by the old-fashioned values of thrift and industry. So you feast and you pick. You dig and you freeze and you put by, until there isn't a clean towel left in the house or an inch of room in the freezer and you're tired of it.

Then it's time to say enough.

It's time to reject remorse, to face down guilt. Need help? Try our five-step peace-of-mind plan:

1. Host a harvest dinner. Get out those dog-eared cookbooks: *101 Ways to Disguise Zucchini* and *52 Ways to Make Tomato Sauce.* Serve a good wine and send leftovers home with the guests.

2. Give away all you can to friends and neighbors. Deliver.

3. Distribute. Leave a box or two on the library steps, near the recycling center at the town dump, in the school parking lot. (We were going to suggest that you stuff zucchini into the mailboxes of everyone on the other side of town, but this is a federal offense. Then again . . .)

4. Feed the compost pile. With this maneuver, you're either feeding the soil or the neighborhood birds and beasts; in either case, you're recycling.

5. Divide leftover tomatoes into even lots and invite a few uninhibited teenagers over for a toss at ten paces. This could prove to be an unforgettable experience, a riotous end to a great gardening year.

Hold That Harvest!

D on't harvest in the face of a storm, old-time gardeners warned. But why?
   It turns out that studies on alfalfa show that plants shift their sugars from stems and leaves to roots in response to a drop in the barometric pressure. So crops picked when a storm is threatening are less nutritious.

Recipes for the Bounty

But wait! If you're too repressed or inhibited — or not quite desperate enough — to resort to the five-step plan, there is another way. Here are a few tried-and-true recipes to help you deal with the last of the crops.

Slide Easy Pickles

Makes about 4 pints.

This is a very old Vermont recipe for sweet cucumber pickles that we obtained from Alice King of Benson, Vermont. Since the cucumbers are seeded and cut up to look a bit like tongues, another name for these pickles is Tongue Pickles. Anyway, they do slide down easy.

ABOUT 8 TO 10 LARGE CUCUMBERS (NO NEED TO USE SMALL PICKLING
CUKES; THIS IS AN END-OF-THE-SEASON RECIPE)
3 CUPS BROWN SUGAR
1½ CUPS MILD WHITE OR CIDER VINEGAR
1 TABLESPOON CASSIA BUDS (OPTIONAL)
1 TABLESPOON WHOLE CLOVES
1 TABLESPOON ALLSPICE BERRIES

1. Peel and slice the cucumbers and cut them into 2- to 3-inch lengths. Soak them overnight in a weak brine (approximately one part salt to ten parts water), then drain.
2. Parboil the cucumbers in equal parts vinegar and water for about 30 minutes, or until they are transparent.
3. Add all the remaining ingredients and cook over medium-high heat, stirring often to prevent sticking, for at least 1 hour, or until they are done.
4. Jar and process as usual.

Confetti Corn Relish

Makes about 6 pints.

A wonderful way to deal with excess sweet corn. Let uneaten corn on the cob accumulate in the refrigerator for a few days, then slice it off the cob and cook up this spicy relish. It's especially tasty served with roast chicken.

2 QUARTS CORN KERNELS (ABOUT 2 DOZEN EARS,
DEPENDING ON SIZE), COOKED
2 CUPS CHOPPED ONIONS
2 CUPS CHOPPED GREEN BELL PEPPERS
2 CUPS CHOPPED RED BELL PEPPERS
2 – 3 FRESH HOT PEPPERS (OR TO TASTE)
1½ CUPS SUGAR
2 TABLESPOONS DRY MUSTARD
1 TABLESPOON CELERY SEEDS
1 TABLESPOON MUSTARD SEEDS
1 TABLESPOON SALT
1 TABLESPOON TURMERIC
3 CUPS VINEGAR
1 CUP WATER

1. Combine all the ingredients in a heavy enamel kettle and simmer for about 45 minutes.
2. Adjust seasonings to taste.
3. Jar and process as usual.

Putting Down Roots

A root cellar is basic technology — a cool, dark place to store root crops without letting them freeze. Root crops (potatoes, carrots, beets, parsnips, turnips, and radishes) like it cool and damp — the higher the humidity, the better. And for long-term storage, nothing suits them better than a place where they can feel right at home: a hole in the earth.

Old-fashioned root cellars were dugouts (sometimes in the side of a hill) with doors, deep enough underground to be frost-free. They provided the necessary darkness and — by occasional opening and closing of the door — ventilation.

Modern takes on the traditional root cellar show considerable ingenuity. If your house has a basement, you can turn a corner of it into a root cellar by insulating the basement ceiling and inside walls. Or, as long as your house has plenty of other exits in case of fire, close off and insulate the bulkhead for the winter months.

Alternatively, if your cellar has an old-fashioned dirt floor, bury a box or barrel in the floor.

If your basement isn't suitable for a root cellar, the backyard alternative is to sink a clean garbage pail into the ground, layer vegetables inside, and mulch thickly for insulation. Finally — and this is very important — mark the spot so you'll be able to find it after the snow falls.

Aunt Sylvia's Zucchini Pancakes

Serves 2 to 3.

Simple, but just the thing for a little lunch. Serve the small pancakes with grated cheese and/or a dab of fresh tomato sauce.

3 CUPS GRATED ZUCCHINI (UNPEELED)
½ CUP FLOUR
1 TEASPOON SALT
½ TEASPOON BAKING SODA
2 EGGS, LIGHTLY BEATEN

1. Squeeze some of the excess water out of the zucchini.
2. Mix the dry ingredients together; combine with the zucchini and eggs.
3. Drop by spoonfuls into a hot, buttered skillet to make pancakes about 2 to 3 inches across. Brown on both sides.
4. Eat hot.

By the Light of the Silvery Moon

Harvest all root vegetables during dry, settled weather, never when the days are cloudy, misty, or rainy. Root crops intended for long-term winter storage should not be dug or pulled up before the autumn leaves begin to fall. Mid-September to Halloween is the best time for most gardeners to harvest crops such as carrots, parsnips, and rutabagas — unless you plan to winter-over the roots in the vegetable garden, tucked in under a thick layer of mulch.

Those who plant according to the phases of the moon are careful to harvest by a parallel set of rules. They recommend gathering fruits and vegetables during the moon's third and fourth quarters, and when it is in a barren sign such as Aquarius, Sagittarius, or Aries. Never harvest, these gardeners counsel, when the moon is in any of the wet signs: Cancer, Scorpio, or Pisces. The water content of growing things is low under the influence of these signs, and that's good, because retained water can cause rot or premature sprouting.

Similarly, when harvesting the seeds from any plant, try to gather them in fair and dry weather, and during the waning of the moon (after the full moon phase but before the next new moon).

When the Man in the Moon says it's time to harvest, do what the man says.

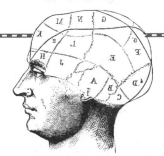

TEST YOUR HARVEST KNOWLEDGE

1 At a traditional cornhusking party, was it considered lucky or unlucky to husk an ear of corn with red kernels?

2 Several of our most popular vegetables are members of the large nightshade family, or Solanaceae. This family also includes some extremely toxic plants, such as bittersweet and deadly nightshade (belladonna). But even our familiar garden crops can be poisonous if eaten in large enough quantities. Which of the following vegetables (commonly eaten parts only) is the most toxic to humans?

a. eggplant
b. tomato
c. green or red pepper
d. Irish potato

3 The first sickles used for harvesting grain were probably developed in ancient Egypt and Babylonia. They had serrated cutting blades and were made of

a. bone.
b. flint.
c. baked clay.
d. bronze.
e. iron.

ANSWERS

1. Lucky, unless you didn't enjoy being kissed. That was the customary reward for finding an ear of red corn. Some farmers even used to "salt" the pile of ears with a few red ones to keep the young people's interest in the work at hand.

2. d. Although all of these vegetables contain chemicals called glycoalkaloids to some extent, potatoes can be the most toxic. An adult who eats 2.4 pounds of potato skins or 3 pounds of whole baking potatoes (about six and a half potatoes) can suffer severe digestive distress if the potatoes were high in glycoalkaloids. Be careful not to eat a potato with a green skin, which indicates the presence of solanine. Also, never eat a shoot from a potato's "eye"; for some varieties, less than an ounce can be highly toxic.

3. c.

PICTURE CREDITS

Planting. 2–3: Library of Congress. 4: North American Bait Farms. Reproduced from *Barrett/Harnessing the Earthworm.* 5: Murray Lemmon/USDA. 6: Movie Still Archives. 8–9: Alan Carey/The Image Works. 9 (top): Shaker Museum and Library, Old Chatham, N.Y.; photo by Lees Studio. 9 (bottom): Hancock Shaker Village. 10–11: Western History Collections, University of Oklahoma. 12: Culver Pictures. 13: Tim McCabe/USDA. 14: Society for the Preservation of New England Antiquities. 17: Massillon Museum. 18: From *Amateur Cultivator's Guide*, 1869, Washburn & Co. Reproduced from *Leighton/American Gardens of the Nineteenth Century.* 21: Movie Still Archives. 22: Everett Collection. 23 (left): Everett Collection. 23 (right): Bettmann Archive. 24–25: Culver Pictures. 26: NASA. 28: Archive Photos/Lambert. 30: Mark Alcarez.

The Weather & Your Garden. 32–33: Bettmann Archive. 34: J. Berndt/The Picture Cube. 36: Culver Pictures. 37: UPI/Bettmann. 38: © Bagdasarian Productions. All rights reserved. 40: USDA. 41: Library of Congress. 42: Everett Collection. 44–45: Culver Pictures. 46: Library of Congress. 47: USDA. 48: State Historical Society of Wisconsin.

Garden Design & Technique. 50–51: USDA. 52–53: Library of Congress. 54–55: White House Historical Association. 56: Rutherford B. Hayes Presidential Center. 57: Stokes Autograph Collection/Yale University Library. 58: White House Historical Association. 59: College of Environmental Design, University of California, Berkeley. 60–61: B. Carrey Collection/The Picture Cube. 62–63: Photo by Darius Kinsey, in *Kinsey, Photographer.* Reproduced from *Conrat/The American Farm.* 66–67: National Archives. 70–71: Dick Lemen. Reproduced from *American Heritage/American Album.* 72: Library of Congress. 74: National Archives. 75: Sara Love.

The Flower Garden. 78–79: Library of Congress. 80: Everett Collection. 82–83: Chrysler Historical Foundation. 86: Michael Ochs Archives. 90: Naval Historical Foundation. 93: David S. Strickler/The Picture Cube. 94–95: Library of Congress. 96–97, 99: Everett Collection. 100: Madelaine Chocolates.

Growing Fruit. 102–103: Nebraska Historical Society. 104–105: © 1939 Turner Entertainment Co. All rights reserved. 107: George

Ulrich. 108: Library of Congress. 110 (top): Chiquita. 110 (bottom): Alan Kamuda/Detroit Free Press. 111: Chiquita. 113: Culver Pictures. 115: National Archives. 116: USDA. 119: David S. Strickler/The Picture Cube. 120–121: Robert Finken/The Picture Cube. 123: Culver Pictures. 125: Welch's. 126: Everett Collection. 127: Massachusetts Historical Society. 128–129: R. P. Kingston Collection/The Picture Cube. 131: Independence National Historic Park. 132: William Huber. 134–135: Washington Rhubarb Growers Association.

The Herb Garden. 138–139: Celestial Seasonings. 140: Ken Hammond/USDA. 141: Gilroy Garlic Festival Association. 142: State Historical Society of Wisconsin. 145: Culver Pictures. 147: Everett Collection. 148: Bettmann Archive. 151: State Historical Society of Wisconsin. 152–153: Everett Collection. 155: Caprilands Herb Farm. 156: Everett Collection. 157: Sara Love. 158–159: National Archives. 162: Ira Kirschenbaum/Stock, Boston.

The Vegetable Garden. 164–165: State Historical Society of Wisconsin. 166: Everett Collection. 168: USDA. 170–171: Barry L. Runk/Grant Heilman Photography. 172: Mr. Potato Head is a registered trademark of Playskool, Inc. 1994. All rights reserved. Used with permission. 174–175: Tim Carlson/Stock, Boston. 177: Bohdan Hrynewych/Stock, Boston. 178–179: USDA. 181: USDA. 182: Everett Collection. 185: Grant Heilman Photography. 187: Thelma Shumsky/Image Works. 188: Courtesy of Vegiforms.

The Harvest. 190–191: Kansas State Historical Society. 192: USDA. 195: Everett Collection. 196–197: British Tourist Authority. 198: Alltrista Consumer Products. 201, 202–203, 204: Library of Congress. 208: Collection of Lee Dennis.

Illustrations on pages 85, 173, 180, and 194 from *Choice Seeds*, 1903 catalog, courtesy of D. V. Burrell Seed Growers Co., Rocky Ford, Colorado.

Note: Diligence was exercised in locating owners of all images used. If an image was uncredited or mistakenly credited, please contact the publisher and effort will be made to include the credit in future printings.